Change, Challenge, and Choices:

Women's Role in Modern Corrections

Edited by Joann B. Morton, D.P.A.

HV
6791
C426
1991

Helen G. Corrothers, President
James A. Gondles, Executive Director
Patricia L. Poupore, Director of Communications and Publications
Elizabeth Watts, Publications Managing Editor
Becky E. Hagenston, Editorial Assistant

ISBN 0-929310-54-3

Printed in the United States of America by St. Mary's Press, Waldorf, Md.

This publication may be ordered from:
American Correctional Association
8025 Laurel Lakes Court
Laurel, Md. 20707-5075
1-800-825-BOOK

Contents

Foreword

Women in recent years have joined the correctional work force in ever-increasing numbers. Their entry into a male-dominated profession has not been without struggle and has resulted in a dramatic change in the complexion of the correctional work force. Knowledge about this change and the challenges of succeeding in a nontraditional work environment have not received the attention they deserve in terms of usable information and strategies for both administrators and employees. This publication is designed to fill that gap.

The American Correctional Association has a long track record of involvement of strong female leadership in the organization. The commitment to assisting and encouraging women in correctional employment continues with the publication of this important and timely work on the subject. The Association plans to continue providing information on this and related topics that will improve and expand the professionalism of the field of corrections. Through the Association's public policies for corrections, accreditation standards, and other activities, we are dedicated to improvement of correctional services throughout the United States and around the world.

James A. Gondles, Jr.
Executive Director
American Correctional Association

Preface

Starting with the Declaration of Principles in 1870, women and the American Correctional Association have been mutually supportive. The Principles urged that "the agency of women be employed" in corrections, and early meetings saw the development of the Women's Correctional Association to develop strategies for implementation of the Principles relative to women employees and offenders. In 1974, the WCA became the Association on Programs for Female Offenders, which focused on a variety of issues particularly relevant to female and juvenile offenders.

Beginning in the 1970s, women employed in corrections reached a number of significant milestones. The Committee on Affirmative Action was formed in 1973. The Women's Caucus, which later evolved into the Women's Task Force, held its first meeting in 1975. In the next year, ACA passed a strong policy statement on affirmative action, and the Women's Task Force was formed three years later. In 1981, guidelines were approved specifying that ACA nominations for officers and board members would be balanced by, among other things, gender. A monograph, *Women in Corrections* (1981), was published incorporating presentations from the first Congress program major track devoted to women employees. In 1987, the Public Correctional Policy on Employment of Women in Corrections was ratified. In 1991, in addition to numerous female Delegate Assembly representatives and committee chairs, women also held the elected offices of president, vice president, treasurer, and eight of the eighteen seats on the Board of Governors.

The Association has benefited from leadership of many women over the years, including Presidents Blanche La Due (1936), Martha Wheeler (1973), Su Cunningham (1987-88), and Helen Corrothers (1991-92); and E. R. Cass recipients Edna Mahan (1963), Catherine Sharp (1974), Martha Wheeler (1977), Marcella Rapp (1982), Lane Murray (1984), Joann Morton (1985), Linda D'Amario Rossi (1988), Su Cunningham (1989), Ruth Rushen (1990), and Diana Travisono (1991). These plus hundreds of other women have greatly enriched the Association and the contribution it has made to corrections.

Joanne B. Morton, D.P.A.

Acknowledgements

Without both the American Correctional Association and the women who have given so much, this publication would not have been possible.

Another key ingredient in the development of this publication was the dedication and professionalism of those friends and associates who contributed their time and talent to prepare material for it. Their unique blend of knowledge and experience, and most of all their willingness to undertake this project on top of their many other responsibilities, was above and beyond the call of duty. Also important were the correctional agencies nationwide who generously answered surveys and questionnaires providing valuable information included in this publication.

Last but not least, a tremendous debt of gratitude is owed to Elizabeth Watts, Managing Editor of ACA, for supporting the concept and "encouraging" its completion; Patricia Watson, Assistant Dean of the College of Criminal Justice at the University of South Carolina, part of whose vacation time was spent expertly reviewing and commenting on the drafts; as well as Nettie Campbell Jacobs, Graduate Research Assistant at the College of Criminal Justice, who with tact and talent processed data and assembled the material into its final form.

Joann B. Morton, D. P. A.

Introduction

Joann B. Morton, D.P.A.

Still grieving for her dead daughter and husband, Mary Weed had no thoughts regarding her place in history when she was appointed to fill her husband's position as warden of Philadelphia's Walnut Street Jail. From 1793 to 1796 she was the first woman to head a correctional facility in the United States (Teeters 1955). This unusual nontraditional role caused some comment even then. La Rochefaucauld described his observations as follows:

> Two hundred eighty prisoners are kept in awe by one woman and four men without arms of any kind, and without dogs . . . keepers are forbidden to carry sticks, lest in a moment of passion they should strike a prisoner, and break in on that system of tranquility and impartial justice, from which is expected so much benefit (Teeters 1955, 47).

The records of the Pennsylvania Prison Society reflected that her tenure was the only time a warden was not accused of malfeasance in office or misappropriation of funds (Teeters 1955).

During the next 200 years, women made numerous contributions in corrections in at least six areas.

1. Women reformers advocated changes in the system (Rafter 1985). They crusaded not only for improvement in programs for women and juveniles but urged reform for male offenders as well.

2. Over the years, women served as chairs and members of governing boards of social service agencies, including corrections. They also championed system improvement as legislators, particularly at the state level (Evans 1989).

3. From the 1800s, women traditionally administered and staffed institutions for women and juveniles as well as provided probation and parole supervision for them as community programs evolved (Freedman 1981).

1

4. Women contributed hundreds of thousands of volunteer hours in all areas of corrections, enriching programs and services throughout the field.
5. For many years, women served in administrative and clerical staff positions throughout the system, often taking on expanded responsibilities for the smooth operation of programs and facilities with little recognition or increase in pay (Rafter & Stanko 1982).
6. In the last twenty years, women have been allowed to begin to participate fully in all areas of corrections and forge careers in so-called nontraditional areas of employment, particularly in male facilities (Zimmer 1986).

This publication was developed to address several areas of need that have evolved with the expanded role of women in correctional employment. Since Title VII of the Civil Rights Act was extended in 1972 to cover governmental employees, correctional agencies have made considerable progress in integrating women into nontraditional jobs in the field. This has not been without controversy however, and this book identifies some of the most critical issues that have emerged dealing with both system and individual changes necessary for successful integration of women in the workplace. It incorporates information that administrators and managers should find useful in successfully building and managing an increasingly heterogeneous work force. Management pitfalls, legal issues, training needs, and other matters relevant to system improvement are addressed. This publication also addresses information, guidelines, and recommendations to assist experienced or neophyte women in correctional employment in maximizing their potential and succeeding in that environment. It should also prove interesting to their male colleagues who wish to broaden their horizons and their knowledge of women in the workplace. Finally, this book contributes to the limited but growing body of knowledge relative to women working in nontraditional environments, specifically that of corrections.

The book is divided into three sections. Part I addresses system issues from several perspectives; Part II provides attention to individual concerns; and Part III deals with the future. While designed in this manner, sections are not mutually exclusive. The reader will find thought-provoking information throughout that should stimulate the improvement of the correctional system and its employees.

Support from top administrators is one key to opening doors for women to enter correctional employment (U.S. Equal Employment Opportunity Commission 1974). Formal and informal channels of communication as well as vigilance by managers must be encouraged if corrections is to make full use of female employees in the workplace. Perry Johnson, with his many years as a correctional administrator, traces his journey through the often turbulent times during the integration of women into the Michigan Department of Corrections. His sensitivity and retroactive analysis of the issues highlight problems that continue to plague the field. Lack of acceptance, sexual harassment, and the need for clear policy and monitoring of practices are viewed with realism and suggest challenges and solutions for others to consider.

The first court case involving women as correctional employees to reach the United States Supreme Court was *Dothard v. Rawlinson* 433 U.S. 321 (1977). A strict adherence to that ruling, which agreed with the Alabama Department of Corrections' exclusion of women from correctional officer positions in male institutions that involved inmate contact, could have precluded the widespread employment of women. However, the ruling was narrowly interpreted across the country as applying only to the particular situation in Alabama, and women began to be employed in many systems. This was not accomplished without a number of other significant legal challenges from several directions. William Collins, an attorney experienced in a wide range of correctional ligation, traces the various legal trends related to employment of women in the field, as well as cross-gender supervision in female facilities, and predicts what direction courts might go in the future.

The most contested area in corrections for employment of women has been that of the correctional officer in male facilities (Zimmer 1986). Joann Morton documents the growth in employment nationally of women officers in male facilities from 1978 to 1988 by both agency and facility security level as well as trends in female facilities. Other data are analyzed, including agencies' changing reasons for hiring women, perceptions of problems and benefits of employing women as correctional officers in male facilities, and limitations placed on them. Recommendations for increased effectiveness in the employment of women in nontraditional roles in corrections are included.

Historically, pregnancy meant termination for women in the workplace. Teachers, nurses, and other professional women often found themselves unemployed as soon as their pregnancy became known. To address this problem, the Pregnancy Discrimination Act of 1979 required that pregnancy be treated like any other temporary disability (U.S. Equal Employment Opportunity Commission 1974). It also specified that pregnancy be addressed in agency policies and procedures. Joann B. Morton reviews the background of the guidelines on pregnancy and their application to corrections.

Another problem area in the integration of women in the workplace has been sexual harassment. While it can occur with either men or women, historically it is more frequent with the latter. Barbara Jones, a correctional agency attorney, defines sexual harassment and provides guidance for administrators and employees on how to prevent sexual harassment or deal with it if it does occur.

Women working in nontraditional environments face a number of challenges. Until recently, female role models were in short supply and neither academic education nor experiential background incorporated the mores and practices needed for success in a predominantly male environment. Rose Etheridge, Cynthia Hale, and Margaret Hambrick's recommendations for succeeding in male institutions are based not only on sound reasoning but also on their experiences as female professionals in male institutions in the early 1980s. Their observations and guidance are as pertinent today as they were then.

Success brings with it stress and often sacrifice. Much has been written about stress and burnout for all employees, as well as women's responsibilities to balance both home and the workplace. Helen Corrothers, a successful corrections professional, reviews the literature and applies it to women in correctional employment. She incorporates a variety of recommendations for successfully coping with stress and burnout from a woman's perspective.

African-American women are playing an increasingly significant role in corrections nationally, yet little study has been done of this issue. Jess Maghan and Leasa McLeish-Blackwell examine this matter as well as study perceptions of African-American women working in corrections in both line and supervisory positions. They provide an interesting and informative perspective as well as strategies that should be applied to maximize African-American women's contributions to the field.

4

Women in corrections have been strong advocates for better services and programs for both juvenile and female offenders. As employment opportunities for women have broadened over the last several years, many women are building their careers in areas dealing with male offenders or the system in general. Without advocates, the needs of the growing number of women offenders are being forgotten. Mary Hawkes traces the history of women's changing role in corrections relative to female offenders and challenges women not to forget female offenders in the future. She predicts that they will have no other voice and, if action is not taken, have the potential to be victims in a system designed only for male offenders.

The final chapter by Joann Morton also focuses on trends that have implications for both the correctional system and the women employees in the future. Recommendations for system improvement, employee enrichment, and future study are included.

References

Evans, S. M. 1989. *Born for liberty*. New York: The Free Press.

Freedman, E. B. 1981. *Their sister's keepers*. Ann Arbor, Mich.: The University of Michigan Press.

Rafter, N. H. 1985. *Partial justice*. Boston: Northeastern University Press.

Rafter, N. H., & E. A. Stanko. 1982. *Judge, lawyer, victim, thief*. Boston: Northeastern University Press.

Teeters, N. K. 1955. *The cradle of the penitentiary: The Walnut Street Jail at Philadelphia, 1773-1835*. Philadelphia: Temple University.

U.S. Equal Employment Opportunity Commission. 1974. *Affirmative action and equal employment, a guidebook for employers*.(2). Washington, D.C.: GPO.

Zimmer, L. E. 1986. *Women guarding men*. Chicago: The University of Chicago Press.

Why Employ Women?

Perry Johnson

Saying anything about the reasons women should be employed in corrections is likely to be redundant because the importance of providing equal opportunity to all in our society is so self-evident. Remembering how ambiguous my own answer to this question had been earlier in my career and realizing that, even today, there is no uniform commitment to fully and appropriately employ women—especially in adult detention facilities and correctional institutions—I recognized that writing this chapter might be more complex and difficult than first imagined. Perhaps, I thought, if I could lead the reader along my own journey, my answer to this question would be more easily understood.

The Beginning

It was a journey commenced some twenty years ago when, as warden of Jackson Prison, I hired its first female officers. It continued through my twelve years as director and on to this day, though my baton has long since passed to others. The road followed was rocky and turbulent—more so for the plucky women who pioneered in this previously all-male domain than for me and the management team.

But there was enough pain to go around. Resistance and sly insubordination by trusted staff—including a warden or two—cruel social and job isolation of women officers by their male counterparts, sexual harassment, and set-ups for failure were unanticipated and troubling barriers. There were lawsuits from inmates, unions, and staff. Some brutal assaults, and even one rape-murder, of female employees may have occurred because of male indifference or perhaps even malice. Was the journey worth the price? Without question. Should women be employed in correctional facilities? By all means.

Some of the issues of twenty years ago are now moot because legal employment rights of women have been defined. However, the two principal reasons for employing women in corrections remain unchanged: the doctrine of fundamental fairness and the need to expand corrections' talent pool.

While we may now clearly see the doctrine of fairness that applies here, it has been a recent insight. In Michigan, as in most states, women were specifically prohibited from working inside the security perimeters of male prisons, from supervising male parolees or probationers, or even from applying for a correctional officer job in a male facility until the early 1970s. And, of course, without entry-level positions for women, there could not be female supervisors within institutions. Racial discrimination, where it existed, was at least unofficial and denied; in the case of women, discrimination based solely on gender was the official policy of the state, of civil service, and of the department. Yet women had for years worked beside officers at information desks and in visiting areas, had been asked to search female visitors, and did it all for clerical pay. Competent and qualified women were denied deserved promotions in other support services at male institutions because "as the boss, they must go inside the walls and deal with inmates."

In field offices, secretarial staff screened and scheduled parolees and probationers, often calming them down until an agent could be found; but no matter how qualified, they could not supervise a caseload of male offenders. The practice was patently unfair, regardless of its legality (it was legally sanctioned at that time), and demanded reform.

A more pragmatic consideration for integrating women into the workplace is corrections' continuing need for competent, qualified workers. If people are excluded solely on the basis of gender, then half of the adult population cannot be considered for this employment, no matter how qualified and motivated they may be. It is a waste of human resources we have never been able to afford. Jackson Prison is a good example. Since its opening in the 1930s, a shortage of qualified correctional officers has been a perennial problem: it was true during the patronage era that led to the Civil Service Act of 1937; it was a significant problem leading to the prison scandals of 1945; it was listed as a major element in the infamous riot of 1952; and it was a factor in a correctional officer mutiny in 1981. Reports following these incidents and similar ones across the nation have noted, among other things, a problem in recruiting qualified and properly motivated correctional officers. How, given this pressing need, can we consider excluding any qualified candidate simply on the basis of gender? We cannot.

When we decided to open to women positions previously restricted to males (known as Bona Fide Occupational Qualification—or BFOQ—in recent years) we simply requested that Civil Service remove the restrictions—giving jus-

7

tification for each. That was the easy part. But how far and how fast should we proceed? Were there special risks for women that we must understand and accommodate? What were the constitutional rights of inmates (privacy and religious rights claims were soon raised by some), and how would they be balanced by the courts against the employment rights of women? What kind of preparation should existing staff have for the change we proposed? We didn't know the answer to these and many other questions because no one had traveled this road before us.

We were fortuitous in selecting the best strategy for the time—incremental implementation. This allowed us to assign women initially to the jobs where we were most certain of success and where they would face the least resistance, both from staff and inmates. Women nurses went to the prison hospitals (women had been prohibited there also); female correctional officers were posted to visiting rooms, towers, gate control, and similar positions. Initially this strategy did not disadvantage women because we always had more positions to fill than candidates. Later this was no longer the case because female correctional officers would need a full range of job experiences for promotion. It was a learning experience for all of us. What we learned and, as important, what we questioned enriched corrections in Michigan. That was an unexpected benefit of integrating women into the workplace.

The Learning Process

Once we decided that women would work in male prisons it was necessary to review our policies and operations from a new perspective. What problems might this cause, and what reasonable accommodations would provide solutions without jeopardizing security? I wish I could say that we thoughtfully and comprehensively planned for this change; we did not. We dealt with the problems as they occurred.

One of the first problems we faced was how to deal with the inmate privacy issue. Visions of the gang showers in the old penitentiaries, prominently situated to provide good visual observation, immediately came to mind. Multiple urinals and totally exposed toilets were suddenly seen in a new light. Some of this heightened social sensibility was no doubt due to a desire to protect women from some of the harsh and demeaning aspects of prison life—in other words, it arose out of chauvinism rather than concern about the feelings of inmates. Eventually, staff designed modesty panels and screens that did not compromise security. Walking around institutions in later years, I was struck with the improvement brought by this simple change. The old way was unnecessarily harsh and demeaning, whether women worked there or not. It was a positive change brought on solely because the need for reasonable accommodation of women forced a new perspective.

The training academy soon brought another concern to our attention: women were failing mandatory rifle qualification at a much higher rate than men. Range officers believed there were two reasons for this: (1) women were more likely to have no prior experience with any weapon, and (2) women were smaller in stature and consequently suffered more from recoil. One obvious solution was to provide more training, and we did; but it also occurred to us that we should review the appropriateness of the weapons we were using. For years we had used heavy .30 calibre rifles on gun towers. These deliver 2,000 to 3,000 foot pounds of energy—enough to kill an elk—and with recoil and muzzle blast to match. Yet the purpose of the weapon was to deter and, when all else failed, to disable to protect life or prevent escape. It was not to "blow people away."

We found that a better option did exist. The one selected was the .223, a civilian adaptation of a military round. It was more accurate, flatter shooting, and less lethal—more effective yet easy to shoot because of its mild recoil and muzzle blast.

Range officers were amazed at the high scores some women were able to achieve with these weapons even on their first shooting experience. The weapons qualification problem was significantly reduced, and better weapons were procured simply because we questioned current practice in our search for reasonable accommodation

Inmate reaction to women officers was a mix of good news and bad news. From the onset, the majority of inmates appeared to welcome the addition of women officers and responded favorably: by most accounts, cursing and obscene language from inmates was toned down in their presence. Women repeatedly told me that inmates were much less of a problem for them than was the hostility of male staff. However, especially in the three old penitentiaries, sexual harassment—both verbal and physical—by some inmates was a problem. It was then that we learned that we had no specific rule against this conduct even though it is among the most offensive and intimidating aspects of prison life, especially for timid inmates. We must insist that officers are respected regardless of gender—but why were we so long insensitive to this problem for inmate victims before women came on board? To deal with this problem, we created a class of infractions termed "sexual misconduct," which prohibits unwanted behavior of a sexual nature. This is another example of the positive effect the introduction of female staff has had on our consciousness.

A few years down the road on this venture I received word that women at one of the institutions were facing insurmountable resistance from male officers and supervisors. I ordered a special internal investigation. It was an eye-opener. The women at this facility were being "frozen out" of the communications network and socially isolated by both officers and supervisors. If it was not for job coaching by well-meaning inmates, they would have been totally lost. The details of the sixty-page report are too lengthy for recitation here, but a listing of some of the lessons learned is useful:

1. The level of opposition by male staff to the integration of women varied dramatically among institutions. This was apparently due to differences in organizational culture, such as officer cliques or tradition. In some cases, individual women were accepted while the concept of women working in the prisons was rejected. Strong personalities were a major factor, with some individuals affecting, either positively or nega-

tively, whole institutions or shifts within the facility. Each situation required individual attention by management to succeed.

2. In large institutions it was necessary to hire a significant number of women as soon as possible so they could develop a mutual support network.

3. Central academy training needed to be followed by on-the-job support that was job-specific to prevent initial training from being undermined by the so-called graybeards.

4. Some system for handling sexual harassment complaints outside facility channels was needed. A responsive hotline to handle complaints was one mechanism, as was a network of experienced women who could assist a complainant in assessing options.

5. Despite the obstacles imposed at the troubled institution, the women were making a valiant effort to do a good job and demonstrated loyalty to the department.

Job Performance Issues

With the advent of female correctional officers inside the security perimeter of prisons, the most often voiced objection from males went like this: "They are increasing the danger for me because they are too small and weak to come to my aid. This also makes them more vulnerable to inmate assault, and I'll have to risk my neck to bail them out more often." Women do tend to be smaller and possess less upper-body strength than men (although the ranges overlap and some women are stronger than some men), so it may be asked if this an important physical attribute they lack.

One means of assessing the importance of individual physical prowess is to study the incidents where force has been used. In doing that, we discovered that in 80 percent of the incidents, force was used to move a recalcitrant inmate only after preparation and mobilization of staff. Since the object was to control the inmate without injury through teamwork, staff for the team were selected for size. This raised another issue for female staff, since experience on cell-rush teams is one aspect of an officer's job not routinely made available to women. This is currently addressed by ensuring that size-appropriate women are included on cell rushes.

In nearly half of the remaining incidents, assaults by inmates followed confrontation and escalation that might have been avoided. There were some incidents of surprise attack, but several staff were usually able to quickly subdue the inmate. The greatest fear of officers is, of course, being the victim of a fatal attack. Three officers, two males and one female, have been murdered by Michigan inmates in this century. Each instance involved a surprise attack where the officers had no opportunity to defend themselves or receive help. We did not uncover any evidence to support the male officers' belief in the importance of physical strength and size.

Another objection to female officers voiced early on by the males was that they were too timid, afraid, emotional, or naive to handle inmates effectively. This has proved not to be the case. Women have demonstrated courage and presence of mind under pressure. Male staff would later grudgingly admit that women tend to be more skillful at defusing hostility than they. The academic achievement and verbal skills of female recruits tended to be higher than for the men; on average, they wrote better reports and communicated more effectively. Were there failures? Of course. Many people, both men and women, do not have the temperament, integrity, or motivation to become good correctional officers, field agents, correctional supervisors, or support staff. Women, however, were no more likely than men to present discipline or job performance problems.

We now have enough experience—nearly twenty years of it—with women working in Michigan's male institutions to welcome their full integration in the work force without reservation. The women who survived their early experiences are now sergeants, lieutenants, captains, inspectors, and wardens. Some are administrative officers, deputy wardens, deputy directors, and some have remained on the line. They bring a slightly different perspective, and their presence in a previously all-male domain has caused a healthy reexamination of cherished beliefs and practices by all. They add to the diversity of ideas and special skills available in the organization that, if recognized, will improve both decision making and performance. But, most of all, they bring a full measure of courage, competence, and loyalty—a welcome addition to any staff.

Legal Issues and the Employment of Women

William C. Collins

As with virtually every other area of change in the field of corrections over the last twenty years, the increasing employment of women in this traditionally male-dominated field has been marked with lawsuits. However, unlike many other areas of correctional development, much of the expansion in the opportunities for women has come not as a result of lawsuits, but almost in spite of them.

This is not to say that concern over laws relating to equal opportunity for women and the obligations those laws create has not been a strong motivating factor in the increase of employment opportunities for women. But most of the case law, at least in the federal courts, has attempted to limit the number of jobs that women could hold in male facilities. Most of this inmate-filed litigation failed. The result has been judicial approval of more and more posts, positions, and functions in which women can perform.

The most dramatic change in correctional job opportunities for women has come in male prisons and jails. For years, these facilities had employed only the smallest number of women in other than traditional clerical or other "women's" tasks. In slightly more than a decade, the doors of those same institutions were opened for women to work in almost every type of job available. (While doors may be officially open, problems remain once inside the doors. Sexual harassment is a serious problem in the correctional workplace, as in most fields. Problems may arise over promotional opportunities. Job qualifications tailored for a male work force may have to be reviewed and changed.)

Dothard v. Rawlinson

The issue of women working in male institutions reached the Supreme Court very early in the era of hands-on court involvement with correctional questions. In 1977 the high court considered *Dothard v. Rawlinson,* which included issues about height and weight requirements for correctional officers working in Alabama's male prisons and a ban on women working

in those maximum security male prisons in what were described as "contact positions."

Not surprisingly, The Supreme Court agreed with the lower court that the height and weight requirements violated Title VII: they disproportionately disqualified women from correctional jobs, and there was no adequate showing by the Alabama Board of Corrections that the requirements were job-related.

What was surprising, however, was the Supreme Court's decision that the ban on women working in the so-called contact positions did not violate Title VII, despite a lower court finding there was no evidence to support the claim that the maximum security prisons posed a *serious* danger to women. The Supreme Court found the dangers in the prison did justify excluding women from them. The Court rested this conclusion partly on findings from other cases dealing with Alabama prisons, which found "junglelike" atmospheres to pervade the institutions.

The decision in *Dothard* produced sharp criticism (Jacobs 1979). But ironically, the decision did not produce a precedent for excluding women from working in male prisons. Perhaps because arguing that *Dothard* justifies excluding women from certain types of facilities is virtually the same as admitting the facilities are unconstitutionally violent, one seldom sees *Dothard* cited in cases involving cross-gender work forces.

As an example of the very limited effect of *Dothard*, consider the results in a Michigan case, *Griffin v. Michigan Department of Corrections*. Women were excluded from working in housing units in three maximum custody facilities (although they could work in housing units in medium and minimum security units). Prison officials attempted to justify the ban on grounds of officer safety and inmate privacy. The district court held flatly that inmates simply did not have any protected constitutional right against being viewed nude by correctional officers of the opposite sex. (Most courts probably would not have taken such an absolute position.) Finding no factual similarity between Michigan prisons and the Alabama institutions, which arguably justified the result in *Dothard*, the court also rejected the safety argument.

Dothard was brought by a woman working in the Alabama system, challenging policies that impeded her employment and advancement. But more commonly the lawsuits in this area are brought by inmates, challenging the presence of women in the institutions.

Are there tasks female correctional officers cannot perform because of excessive intrusion into male inmates' legitimate expectations of privacy? How can the interests of women in equal opportunity be weighed and balanced against the competing interests inmates have in avoiding being seen by persons of the opposite sex while showering, using the toilet, and changing clothes? These are the typical questions courts have had to deal with in cross-gender work force lawsuits.

The results of these cases have shifted over the years. In general, the shift has been one that has opened up more and more posts to women and has required less and less that institution administrators accommodate the interests of both the women seeking work and inmates seeking privacy.

The Early Cases: Accommodation

In *Reynolds v. Wise* (1974), one of the earliest decisions, a Texas district court ruled that excluding women from working in male prison dormitories reasonably accommodated inmate privacy interests and did not discriminate against the women.

Undercutting any arguments that assumed inmates enjoyed strong privacy interests was *Hudson v. Palmer*, a Supreme Court case decided in July 1984. While dealing with cell searches, not female officers, the case held that inmates had no reasonable expectation of privacy in their cells and cell contents. This result became, in essence, the benchmark against which all inmate privacy claims would be measured. By setting the benchmark as low as possible (no expectation of privacy, as opposed to some limited privacy interest), the Court gave advocates of inmate privacy interests in almost any context a tougher row to hoe in order to succeed in litigation.

But even before *Hudson*, lower courts were recognizing that the equal employment interests of women demanded they be allowed to work in male prisons. At first the court tried to reduce the intrusion on male inmate privacy by demanding the institution administration develop ways of accommodating both the expanded female work force and inmate privacy. In *Hardin v. Stynchcomb*, the court ordered officials to erect privacy screens and to juggle work schedules to increase the number of positions women could work. In *Percy v. Allen* (1982), the Maine Supreme Court ruled that selective job assignments had to be at least considered before women could be excluded from most positions in a male institution.

During the latter half of the 1980s, courts moved away from the accommodation posture and more commonly held that limited observation of male inmates in the nude by female correctional officers simply does not violate any rights of the inmates, nor does it require any exceptional actions by institution officials to physically modify the institution or juggle work schedules.

Perhaps the leading case dealing with female officers and male inmates is *Grummett v. Rushen*, which arose from San Quentin. Women worked virtually everywhere in San Quentin, one of California's highest security prisons. Officers (including women) could see into cells (each cell had a toilet) from tiers directly in front of the cells and from gunwalks. At least one common shower area was observable. While women did not conduct or observe strip searches (except in emergency situations), they did perform routine pat searches, which included contact with the groin area.

Where the observation of nude inmates was "infrequent and casual . . . or from a distance," no privacy rights of the inmates were violated, even though the court felt inmate privacy rights could be restricted only on the basis of a "compelling state interest" (779 F.2d at 494). Similarly, the pat searches violated no rights of the inmates, assuming that the searches were done in a professional manner.

Religious objections to cross-gender pat searches have been made with varying results. In *Madyun v. Franzen*, the Seventh

Circuit court of appeals upheld cross-gender pat searches over religious objections by Muslim inmates, while a New York state appellate court reached the opposite conclusion in *Rivera v. Smith.*

The Court of Appeals for the Eighth Circuit (Iowa, Arkansas, Missouri, Minnesota, Nebraska, and the Dakotas) also followed the Ninth Circuit's lead in approving both casual observation and pat searches of male inmates by female officers (*Timm v. Gunter*). The court felt that whatever privacy interests the inmates may have had were overcome by the interests of the institution in maintaining security and in furthering the goal of equal employment opportunity. Inmates were able to keep opposite sex observation of them to a minimum by being careful of how they stood in the shower and by judicious use of towels. In sharp contrast to earlier accommodation cases, the court recognized the problems that could be created by restricting women to day shifts (when more staff was around) or creating a number of single sex posts, and they reversed the trial court's requirement that female officers' schedules be arranged around inmate privacy interests.

The approach taken by the court in *Timm*, which balances the inmates' privacy interests against the legitimate interests of the institution, is the approach other courts will take in evaluating this sort of claim. In defending the use of cross-gender supervision, it is incumbent on the institution to demonstrate what interests it has in a cross-gender work force, the alternatives the inmates have to maintain their privacy, the impact on the institution's interests (including budget and staffing) if the inmates' requests are accommodated, and that there are no obvious, ready alternatives to the cross-gender approach the institution has chosen.

Cross-gender In Female Facilities

The cross-gender pat search issue, although largely resolved for women working in male facilities, remains unsettled for men working in female facilities. This issue has arisen rarely; however, at least three courts, looking at different factual situations at different times during the evolution of correctional law, all have tended to favor the female inmates' privacy over competing interests of the institution. Most recently, in *Jordan v. Gardner,* a federal district court in Washington found a cross-gender pat search policy in a women's prison to violate rights of some or all inmates under the First (freedom of religion), Fourth (unreasonable search), and Eighth (cruel and unusual punishment) Amendments. *Jordan* has been appealed, and a decision is likely during 1991.

Several factors appear to have come together to support the dramatic expansion of posts and functions that women may perform throughout corrections. Two are the concept of equal opportunity and society's recognition that there is no legitimate reason to exclude women from most jobs in any profession. Another is the increasing willingness of the courts to recognize, defer to, and uphold legitimate interests of institution administrators, even though those interests may restrict constitutional freedoms of offenders.

Tasks that involve extraordinary intrusions into one's privacy—such as performing strip searches—probably remain limited to same-sex officers. But such tasks are not so common as to seriously limit the number of posts available to women in corrections. There may be forces that continue to limit the real ability of women to enter corrections and advance up a career ladder, but legal constraints coming from concerns about inmate privacy should not be counted among these.

Reference

Jacobs. 1989. The sexual integration of the prison's guard force: A few comments on *Dothard v. Rawlinson*. 10 *Toledo Law Review* 389 (Winter).

Court Cases

Griffin v. Michigan Department of Corrections, CA No. 80-71516 (E.D. Mich., 1083, unreported).

Grummett v. Rushen, 779 F.2d 491 (9th Cir., 1985).

Hardin v. Stynchcomb, 691 F.2d 1364 (11th Cir., 1982).

Hudson v. Palmer, 104 S.Ct. 3194 (1984).

Jordan v. Gardner, C-89-339 TB, March 6, 1990, unreported.*

Madyun v. Franzen, 704 F.2d 954 (7th Cir., 1985)

Percy v. Allen, 449 A.2d 337 (Me., 1982).

Pugh v. Locke, 406 F. Supp. 318, 323-325 (M.D. Ala., 1976).

Reynolds v. Wise, 375 F.Supp. 145 (N.D. Texas, 1974).

Rivera v. Smith, 462 NYS2d 352 (App., 1983).

Timm v. Gunter, 913 F.2d 1093 (8th Cir., 1990).

Turner v. Safley 107 S.Ct. 2254 (1987).

---

* *A discussion of this case appears at 11* Correctional Law Reporter *34 (July 1990). See also* Torres v. Wisconsin Department of Health and Social Services, *838 F.2d 944 (7th Cir., 1988),* Forts v. Ward, *621 F.2d 1210, (2nd Cir., 1980)* .

Women Correctional Officers: A Ten-year Update

Joann B. Morton, D.P.A.

Over the last forty years one of the most significant changes in the American work force has been the increasing number of women working outside the home. In 1948, one third of all women over sixteen years old were in the workplace; by 1988, that number had risen to 56.6 percent. In contrast, the percentage of men sixteen years of age and over in the work force dropped from 86.6 percent to 76.2 percent during the same time frame (U.S. Department of Labor 1989).

Women have traditionally been under-represented in the correctional workplace. The Joint Commission on Correctional Manpower and Training in 1969 noted that while women made up 40 percent of the general work force, they accounted for only 12 percent of the correctional work force (American Correctional Association 1981). In 1979, women accounted for 42 percent of the labor force but only 29.3 percent of the correctional employees (Chapman 1983).

By 1990, the number of women employed in corrections had increased to an overall rate of 43 percent. Probation and parole agencies led the way with 52 and 50 percent female workers respectively. Juvenile agencies had 42 percent; adult institutional agencies with 28 percent had the lowest level of female employees (Camp & Camp 1990).

The low percentage of women in adult correctional institutions may have been a reflection of the lack of full integration of women into positions of correctional officers in male facilities, which make up a large proportion of the job opportunities in this field. However, the employment of women—particularly as correctional officers in male facilities—began to increase rapidly when the 1972 Title VII of the Civil Rights Act was amended to include state and local governmental personnel practices (Morton 1979).

Methodology

This article compares the results of two similar surveys of women correctional officers in male facilities, one conducted in 1978 (Morton 1979) and one ten years later. As in 1978, a

19

survey was mailed to administrators of state adult correctional agencies and the Federal Bureau of Prisons listed in the 1989 American Correctional Association's *Juvenile and Adult Correctional Departments, Institutions, Agencies, and Paroling Authorities.* The survey requested information as of December 1988. A second mailing was made to those who did not respond initially, and in some instances telephone follow-up was made to clarify survey information. Surveys were submitted by 45 states and the Federal Bureau of Prisons for a 90 percent rate of return. In some instances, responses were not complete and are so noted in the analysis.

Number of Female Officers

In 1988, women made up 12.9 percent of the correctional officer work force in male correctional facilities—almost double the 6.6 percent reported in 1978. Table 1 lists the 45 states' and the Federal Bureau of Prisons' responses in rank order by the percentage of women officers in male facilities compared to that in 1978.

Mississippi, the only state not reporting in 1978, was ranked first in 1988, with 36.1 percent female officers in male facilities. South Carolina, ranked fifth in 1978, had almost doubled its percentage to 24.9 percent in 1988 and ranked second nationally. North Dakota, ranked fifteenth in 1978, advanced to third in 1988. Indiana, which ranked twelfth in 1978, more than doubled the percentage of women correctional officers employed in male facilities in 1988 to rank fourth.

In 1978, four states—Alaska, Pennsylvania, Texas, and Utah—reported that they did not hire women as correctional officers in male facilities. By 1988, two of those states, Alaska and Texas, were ranked fifth and sixth nationally in the percentage of female officers they employed in their male facilities. At the other end of the scale in 1988, North Carolina, Pennsylvania, and Rhode Island reported employing less than 5 percent female correctional officers in their male facilities.

While the issues of women working in male facilities have received some attention in recent years, there has been limited attention concerning women working in female facilities. This study indicated an interesting change of employment patterns in female institutions during this ten-year time span.

As Table 2 demonstrates, in 1978 women accounted for 83 percent of the officers in female institutions while men accounted for 17 percent. Eight agencies reported they did not hire male officers in their female facilities. By 1988, the per-

20

centage of women officers in female facilities had dropped to 65.2 percent, with a corresponding rise in the percentage of male officers to an average of 34.8 percent. Only three agencies indicated they had no male officers in their female facilities, and twelve agencies reported less than 50 percent female officers compared to only one such agency in 1978.

The decrease in employment of women in female facilities was greatly offset by the increased opportunities for women to work in male facilities. Most agencies only had one female facility, so the number of correctional officer positions in such facilities was limited. Of the positions accounted for in the study, those available in male facilities outnumbered those in female facilities by over 94,000. Out of a total of 98,678 correctional officer positions in male facilities, 12,691 were filled by women. This compared to 2,996 female correctional officers out of a possible 4,598 in female facilities. These numbers reinforce the disparate impact that limiting employment in male facilities would have on women.

Women's Role Expands

It might be assumed that women would be employed in lower level security facilities at a much greater rate than they would in high or maximum security male facilities. This would be the case particularly if there were concerns about the safety of female officers in higher security institutions or their ability to manage maximum security inmates. The 1978 survey found that women on the average were indeed employed in minimum security at almost twice the percentage (9 percent) as they were in medium security (5 percent) or maximum security (4 percent).

By 1988, as Table 3 demonstrates, the differences in the average employment rates by security level were much less evident. Overall, women made up 12.7 percent of the correctional officer positions in male maximum security facilities. Agencies reported a high of 21.6 percent in Nevada to zero percent in Arkansas and the Federal Bureau of Prisons. In medium security male facilities there was an average of 13.4 percent female employment, and in minimum there was an average of 14.7 percent female employment. Only Maine reported women were not employed in medium security, and Alabama reported no women employed in minimum security facilities.

The reasons for hiring women as correctional officers in male facilities also reflected some of the changes that have taken place over the last ten years. When the initial survey

Table 1
Comparison of Employment of Female COs in Male Facilities, 1978-1988

1988 Rank	State	Total # COs	# M COs	# F COs	% F COs (1978)	1978 Rank	% F COs (1988)
1	Miss.	1,022	653	369	36.1	**	**
2	S. C.	2,671	2,006	665	24.9	5	13.9
3	N. D.	100	78	22	22.0	15	8.1
4	Ind.	1,912	1,557	355	18.6	12	8.5
5	Alaska	583	480	103	17.7	*	*
6	Tex.	8,301	6,877	1,424	17.2	*	*
7	Wash.	1,594	1,328	266	16.7	22	5.4
8	Tenn.	2,147	1,805	342	15.9	26	4.7
9	La.	2,732	2,302	430	15.7	1	18.2
10	Mich.	7,802	6,588	1,214	15.6	8	12.5
11	Calif.	9,057	7,653	1,404	15.5	10	9.8
12	Colo.	875	745	130	14.9	27	4.6
13	Va.	3,567	3,038	529	14.8	9	10.7
14	Kan.	1,115	950	165	14.8	6	12.6
15	Ky.	1,080	925	155	14.4	3	15.9
16	Minn.	856	738	118	13.8	17	7.2
17	Ohio	3,301	2,846	455	13.8	28	4.6
18	Ore.	385	332	53	13.8	23	5.4
19	Neb.	371	322	49	13.2	30	4.2
20	Vt.	215	187	28	13.0	18	6.7
21	Okla.	1,102	964	138	12.5	4	13.9
22	Mass.	1,584	1,393	191	12.1	35	3.0
23	Ga.	3,595	3,189	406	11.3	24	4.8

1988 Rank	State	Total # COs	# M COs	# F COs	% F COs (1988)	1978 Rank	% F COs (1978)
24	N.Y.	14,283	12,683	1,600	11.2	34	3.2
25	Mo.	2,132	1,899	233	10.9	13	8.4
26	N.H.	211	188	23	10.9	31	4.2
27	Hawaii	596	533	63	10.6	**	**
28	Del.	604	541	63	10.4	14	8.2
29	Wis.	1,375	1,233	142	10.3	25	4.7
30	Nev.	438	394	44	10.1	7	12.6
31	Utah	287	259	28	9.8	*	*
32	Idaho	195	176	19	9.7	21	5.6
33	Ill.	5,369	4,855	514	9.6	11	9.3
34	Ark.	760	690	70	9.2	29	4.5
35	W. Va.	349	317	32	9.2	37	2.9
36	Ala.	1,697	1,544	153	9.0	20	6.2
37	Iowa	743	688	55	7.4	16	7.3
38	Maine	217	202	15	6.9	44	0.0
39	FBP, D.C.	4,611	4,299	312	6.8	n/a	n/a
40	Conn.	1,500	1,423	77	5.1	39	1.7
41	R.I.	521	498	23	4.4	43	0.0
42	Penn.	2,892	2,798	94	3.3	*	*
43	N. C.	3,931	3,811	120	3.1	33	4.0
44	Ariz.	**	**	**	**	41	1.4
45	Fla.	**	**	**	**	38	2.8
46	Mont.	**	**	**	**	42	0.6
	TOTAL	98,678	85,987	12,691	12.9		6.6

* Responded in 1978 they did not hire women as COs in male facilities.
** No response or data not usable.

Table 2
Comparison of Employment of Female COs in Female
Facilities, 1978-1988

1988 Rank	State	Total # COs	# M COs	# F COs	% of F COs (1988)	1978 Rank	% F COs (1978)
1	Ark.	49	0	49	100.0	29	100.0
2	Del.	21	0	21	100.0	10	74.0
3	Maine	4	0	4	100.0	*	
4	Minn.	52	1	51	98.1	21	88.0
5	La.	125	3	122	97.6	29	98.0
6	Ore.	32	1	31	96.9	24	91.0
7	Ga.	142	10	132	93.0	16	79.0
8	S. C.	120	12	108	90.0	14	75.0
9	Ind.	119	16	103	86.6	20	81.0
10	Ill.	217	33	184	84.8	9	72.0
11	Va.	85	13	72	84.7	17	79.0
12	Ky.	56	9	47	83.9	12	74.0
13	Colo.	31	5	26	83.9	29	100.0
14	N. C.	181	35	146	80.7	7	70.0
15	N. D.	10	2	8	80.0	30	100.0
16	Conn.	149	32	117	78.5	8	71.0
17	Ala.	79	19	60	76.0	18	80.0
18	Tex.	565	142	423	74.9	*	
19	Neb.	25	7	18	72.0	23	90.0
20	Penn.	200	56	144	72.0	13	74.0
21	Ohio	210	62	148	70.5	15	78.0
22	Wis.	82	27	55	67.1	2	63.0
23	Mass.	121	43	78	64.5	*	

1988 Rank	State	Total # COS	# M COs	# F COs	% F COs (1988)	1978 Rank	% F COs (1978)
24	Tenn.	166	62	104	62.7	5	67.0
25	Nev.	35	14	21	60.0	11	74.0
26	Iowa	47	19	28	59.6	29	100.0
27	R. I.	42	17	25	59.5	*	
28	Utah	21	9	12	57.1	30	100.0
29	Wash.	69	35	34	49.3	1	45.0
30	Mo.	65	33	32	49.2	*	
31	Cal.	333	176	157	47.2	3	64.0
32	Mich.	355	193	162	45.6	27	92.0
33	FBP, D.C.	258	148	110	42.6	n/a	n/a
34	Kans.	51	32	19	37.3	10	74.0
35	W. Va.	17	11	6	35.3	30	100.0
36	Idaho	6	4	2	33.3	**	
37	N. Y.	319	213	106	33.2	26	91.0
38	Okla.	43	31	12	27.9	19	81.0
39	Vt.	48	38	10	20.8	**	
40	Hawaii	48	39	9	18.8	*	
41	Alaska	*	*	*	*	22	88.0
42	Ariz.	*	*	*	*	28	98.0
43	Fla.	*	*	*	*	6	69.0
44	Miss.	*	*	*	*	*	
45	Mont.	*	*	*	*	**	
46	N. H.	*	*	*	*	**	
	TOTAL	4,598	1,602	2,996	65.2		83.0

* Data on this question not reported or unusable.

** Idaho, Maine, Montana, New Hampshire, Vermont, Wyoming reported no separate female institutions in 1978.

Table 3
1988 Percentage of Female COs by Male Facility Security Level

State	MAXIMUM			MEDIUM			MINIMUM		
	Total COs	# of F COs	% of F COs	Total COs	# of F COs	% of F COs	Total COs	# of F COs	% of F COs
Alabama	670	13	1.9	845	121	14.3	67	0	0.0
Alaska	177	23	12.0	406	80	19.7	—	—	—
Arizona	—	—	—	—	—	—	—	—	—
Arkansas	116	0	0.0	505	45	8.9	75	14	18.6
California	3,337	506	15.0	4,550	745	16.3	1,170	153	13.0
Colorado	185	24	12.9	571	90	15.7	119	16	13.4
Connecticut	370	15	4.0	996	56	5.6	134	6	4.4
Delaware	568*	63*	11.0*	—	—	—	36	0	0.0
Florida	—	—	—	—	—	—	—	—	—
Georgia	547	97	17.7	155	20	12.9	—	—	—
Hawaii	117	7	5.9	479	56	11.6	—	—	—
Idaho	—	—	—	153	11	7.1	36	6	16.6
Illinois	2,127	191	8.9	2,300	227	9.8	872	74	8.4
Indiana	688	41	5.9	1,126	290	25.5	—	—	—
Iowa	303	17	5.6	383	31	8.0	57	7	12.2

State	MAXIMUM			MEDIUM			MINIMUM		
	Total COs	# of F COs	% of F COs	Total COs	# of F COs	% of F COs	Total COs	# of F COs	% of F COs
Kansas	812	112	13.7	154	25	16.2	149	28	18.7
Kentucky	242	28	11.5	680	117	17.2	158	10	6.3
Louisiana	1,140	169	14.8	456	241	52.8	—	—	—
Maine	156	9	5.7	25	0	0.0	26	4	15.3
Massachusetts	198	14	7.0	1,338	173	12.9	48	4	8.3
Michigan	1,638	228	13.9	5,682	928	16.3	482	58	12.0
Minnesota	643	74	11.5	70	10	14.2	143	34	23.7
Mississippi	—	—	—	185	29	15.6	837	340	40.6
Missouri	583	79	13.5	1,290	112	8.6	202	29	14.3
Montana	—	—	—	—	—	—	—	—	—
Nebraska	177	23	12.9	141	16	11.3	53	10	18.8
Nevada	37	8	21.6	336	30	8.9	55	3	5.4
New Hampshire	30	5	16.6	156	16	10.2	19	1	5.2
New York	6,875	706	10.2	6,475	791	12.2	564	61	10.8
North Carolina	1,463	76	5.1	1,405	21	1.4	1,063	23	2.1
North Dakota	85*	19*	22.3*	—	—	—	15	3	20.0
Ohio	1,313	109	8.3	1,777	311	17.5	162	27	16.6
Oklahoma	237	36	15.1	593	77	12.9	205	15	7.3

27

Table 3 — continued

State	MAXIMUM			MEDIUM			MINIMUM		
	Total COs	# of F COs	% of F COs	Total COs	# of F COs	% of F COs	Total COs	# of F COs	% of F COs
Oregon	251	33	13.1	120	17	14.1	14	3	21.4
Pennsylvania	993	39	3.9	1,899	55	2.8	—	—	—
Rhode Island	328	17	5.1	104	4	3.8	56	1	1.7
South Carolina	1,972*	497*	25.2*	—	—	—	638	153	23.9
Tennessee	705	96	13.6	1,210	200	16.5	116	23	19.8
Texas	8,301	1,424	17.1	—	—	—	—	—	—
Utah	—	—	—	—	—	—	—	—	—
Vermont	—	—	—	—	—	—	—	—	—
Virginia	2,838	464	16.3	719	64	8.9	—	—	—
Washington	1,031	141	13.6	447	100	22.3	81	15	18.5
West Virginia	208	19	9.1	112	6	5.3	20	5	25.0
Wisconsin	771	78	10.1	358	36	10.0	108	23	21.0
TOTAL	42,232	5,500	12.8	38,201	5,151	13.4	7,780	1,149	14.7
FBP	883	0	0.0	2,772	215	7.7	956	97	10.1

*Maximum and medium correctional facilities combined.

Note: Data from Arizona, Florida, Montana, Utah, and Vermont not available.

was conducted in 1978, equal employment opportunity for women and minorities had strong support from the federal government. Seminars and workshops were being conducted nationwide for governmental managers explaining the legal requirement of Title VII of the Civil Rights Act and the guidelines issued by the Equal Employment Opportunity Commission (EEOC). This emphasis was mirrored by the overwhelming majority of agencies, which in 1978 reported hiring women because of equal employment mandates. By 1988, almost half of the agencies were beginning to reflect both the changing emphasis on equal employment opportunities and the shortage of male applicants by hiring women because of workforce/management-related reasons.

One of the issues raised in the conclusion of the 1978 study that merited more research was how women officers were being deployed in male facilities around the country. If they were denied access to inmate contact positions, then their opportunity for advancement in the security ranks would be severely limited. Also, since the 1978 study reflected a strong concern by correctional administrators about "inmate privacy" for male offenders, it was predicted that this attitude could limit women's employment opportunities. By 1988, thirty-four agencies indicated they had limits on female officers functioning in male facilities compared to eleven who did not limit women. Only one agency limited men in female institutions but not women in male facilities. The rule appeared to be if you limited women you also limited men. However, as previously noted, limits placed on women in male facilities can have a serious impact numerically on employment opportunities for women, while limits on men in female facilities can have little effect on their employment opportunities.

In 1988, the limitations varied from Delaware, where officers were prohibited by law from manning posts in housing areas of the opposite sex, to the more common narrow limitations of strip searching inmates of the opposite sex and collecting urine samples. All of the limitations dealt with some aspect of inmate privacy, and none dealt with safety and security of the institutions or safety or ability of the female officers. (See Table 4.)

Problems and Benefits

Inmates' right to privacy was cited as a problem agencies were having using women as correctional officers in male facilities. Seventeen states in 1988 reported that their major problems with employing women correctional officers in male

Table 4
Limitations on Female Officers in Male Facilities and
Male Officers in Female Facilities

State	Limitations on Female Officers	Limitations on Male Officers
Alabama	strip searches/ pat downs	strip searches/ pat downs
Alaska	work only relief in facilities	work only relief in facilities
Arizona	strip searches	strip searches
Arkansas	direct inmate contact	no male applicant
California	security housing	security housing
Colorado	no limitations	housing area
Connecticut	based on inmate privacy	based on inmate privacy
Delaware	housing area	housing area
Florida	strip searches	strip searches
Georgia	no limitations	no limitations
Hawaii	no limitations	no limitations
Idaho	no limitations	no limitations
Illinois	open showers & toilets/ strip searches	open showers & toilets/ strip searches
Indiana	strip searches	strip searches
Iowa	strip searches	strip searches
Kansas	no limitations	no limitations
Kentucky	restrooms/ shower area	restrooms/ shower area
Louisiana	no limitations	no limitations
Maine	housing/ strip searches	housing/ strip searches
Massachusetts	strip searches	strip searches
Michigan	no limitations	no limitations
Minnesota	two posts are male only	housing/cottages
Mississippi	no limitations	no limitations

State	Limitations on Female Officers	Limitations on Male Officers
Missouri	no response	no response
Montana	no limitations	no limitations
Nebraska	pat downs/ showers/housing	pat downs/ showers
Nevada	no limitations	no limitations
New Hampshire	searches	searches
New York	strip searches/ showers	strip searches/ showers
North Carolina	dormitories/ privacy	dormitories/ privacy
North Dakota	searches/ medical	searches/ pat downs/ medical
Ohio	contact posts	no response
Oklahoma	searches/ urine collection	searches/ urine collection
Oregon	searches/ showers & toilets	searches/ showers & toilets
Pennsylvania	searches/ showers/medical	searches/ showers/medical
Rhode Island	discretion used	body searches
South Carolina	searches/ showers	searches/ showers
Tennessee	no limitations	no limitations
Texas	body cavity searches	body cavity searches
Utah	strip searches	strip searches
Vermont	strip searches	strip searches
Virginia	BFOQ rules	BFOQ rules
Washington	skin & strip searches	skin & strip searches
West Virginia	strip searches	n/a
Wisconsin	strip searches/ urine	strip searches/ urine
FBP	strip searches and level 5	strip searches

facilities were ensuring inmate privacy or staff scheduling problems that were related to ensuring privacy. The agencies were equally divided in the two other problem areas noted. Seven listed acceptance and sexual harassment by male staff, and seven listed inappropriate conduct between male inmates and female officers. On the other hand, in female institutions no agency listed acceptance of male officers as a problem. Eight cited privacy issues, and seven cited scheduling issues that might be related to privacy as problems with male officers in female facilities. Ten noted inappropriate behavior of male officers, including sexual harassment of female inmates. Only one agency, Wisconsin, reflected a concern about the security and the rehabilitation of the female inmates with male officers having full access to the population.

On the positive side, perceptions of the benefits of hiring women fell into four main categories. The benefit cited by more than half of the agencies was related to inmate management and the institutional climate. Comments such as women officers have a "calming effect," "inmates and staff are better behaved," and "security is improved" were typical responses. Seven agencies cited an expanded manpower pool, and the same number cited normalizing the institutional environment to reflect the outside world as positive benefits of having women correctional officers in their male facilities. Three agencies responded that women made better employees.

Fewer responses were received for advantages of hiring men in female facilities. In that area, eleven agencies cited the institutional environment as a positive factor, but the emphasis was on men serving as "role models" for the female offenders.

Another area explored was whether agencies provided training to assist women officers working in male facilities. Twenty-two agencies reported that they did provide some type of specialized training to assist women officers in coping in male facilities. Twenty-two agencies indicated that they did not provide any specialized training other than that available to all employees.

The litigious nature of society and corrections has meant that the road to full employment of women has not been without problems. In all, thirty-one agencies reported they had grievances or court cases filed involving male or female officers working in opposite-sex facilities. Thirteen involved both sexes, seventeen involved female correctional officers working in male facilities, and one involved males working in a female facility. The grievances and court cases were filed by inmates, staff, and outside agencies, including the federal government, which initiated affirmative action suits in several states. Fifteen agencies reported they had no grievances or court cases involving officers in opposite-sex facilities. Table 5 reflects information received on both training and grievance/court cases.

In looking toward the future, the agencies were over-whelmingly positive in their predictions for the increased employment of women in male facilities. Thirty-three of the thirty-nine agencies responding to this question reported that they planned to expand the number of women correctional officers in male facilities, and several noted that they felt women's roles would continue to include more movement of females into supervisory positions in those institutions.

Conclusions

Women have narrowed the gap between their representation in the general work force (56.6 percent) and their level of employment in corrections (43 percent). And while their rate of employment as correctional officers in male facilities did not approach that of their employment rate in either the general or the correctional work force, it had almost doubled from 6.6 percent in 1978 to 12.9 percent in 1988.

The growth was not consistent across the country. Some agencies made great strides in the percentage of women employed while others remained the same or lost ground. There was no single reason for this inconsistency. It was a reflection of the diverse nature of correctional organizations nationally as well as the changing nature of correctional leadership and priorities established by agency heads. Man-power needs, attention by the federal courts, union involvement, economic conditions, and even historical and sociological influences were only a few of the other factors that might have influenced these trends. States that were side by side and shared many common characteristics, such as North Carolina and South Carolina, were on opposite ends of the scale. The Federal Bureau of Prisons, which has taken the lead in so many areas of corrections, surprisingly ranked thirty-ninth out of forty-six agencies responding in employment of women in male facilities. Only two responding agencies did not employ females as officers in male maximum security facilities. Why these differences exist is certainly a fertile area of additional research.

One pattern was clear, however: increasingly, correctional agencies were becoming dependent on women to make up a

Table 5
Report of Court Cases/Grievances and Training

State	Court Cases/Grievances				Special Training for Female Officers in Male Facilities	
	Both Sexes	Female Only	Male Only	None	Yes	No
Alabama	*					*
Alaska				*		*
Arizona		*			*	
Arkansas						
California				*	*	
Colorado			*		*	
Connecticut		*				*
Delaware		*				*
Florida	*				*	
Georgia	*					*
Hawaii				*		*
Idaho		*				*
Illinois		*			*	
Indiana		*			*	
Iowa		*			*	
Kansas				*		*
Kentucky				*		*
Louisiana				*		*
Maine	*					*
Massachusetts	*					*
Michigan	*					*
Minnesota		*			*	
Mississippi				*		*

State	Court Cases/Grievances				Special Training for Female Officers in Male Facilities	
	Both Sexes	Female Only	Male Only	None	Yes	No
Missouri				*	*	
Montana				*		*
Nebraska						
Nevada		*			*	
New Hampshire	*					*
New York	*				*	
North Carolina				*		*
North Dakota		*			*	
Ohio		*			*	
Oklahoma		*				*
Oregon	*				*	
Pennsylvania	*				*	
Rhode Island		*				*
South Carolina		*			*	
Tennessee				*	*	
Texas		*				*
Utah				*	*	
Vermont	*				*	
Virginia				*		*
Washington				*	*	
West Virginia						
Wisconsin	*				*	
FBP		*			*	

significant percentage of the officer work force in male facilities. The decreasing number of available male applicants and increasing number of women entering employment were demographic trends reflected in corrections as well as other labor-intensive organizations. These factors, which helped overcome the low priority the enforcement of Title VII of the Civil Rights Act received from the federal government in the 1980s, have the potential to be a more positive influence on the employment of women than litigation. If women are hired because they are needed for the ongoing success of the organization, they may be better received and more effectively deployed.

The decrease in the percentage of women officers in female facilities was an interesting by-product of equal opportunity employment. It has often been overlooked that men have always worked in most female facilities. They made up over 17 percent of the officer work force in female facilities in 1978 and increased to 35 percent by 1988. Early crusaders for separate facilities for women inmates argued that women needed to be supervised by women because of the history of abuse of women inmates by both male inmates and staff. It was significant that only one state, Wisconsin, acknowledged a concern for the impact that the use of male officers might have on the rehabilitation of female inmates. The majority of agencies reported hiring men in female institutions because of equal employment requirements. However, with respect to Title VII, initially nonminority men were not a "covered class" who had equal employment rights under the act since their employment opportunities had not been limited. On the other hand, limiting women's employment opportunities in male facilities had a tremendous disparate effect numerically on them and thus were addressed under the act. The effects of increased numbers of male officers in female facilities requires additional study. Its success or failure in the long run will probably reflect the sensitivity of institutional managers and the training staff receive.

Another interesting finding was the balanced use of female officers among the different levels of security, from maximum to medium to minimum. It appears that most correctional agencies had resolved whatever problems had existed earlier with employing women in male maximum security facilities. Again there was inconsistency around the country that might have resulted from any number of factors. Regardless of the causes, employing women as correctional officers in male maximum security facilities will enhance the opportunity for advancement of women for at least the following three reasons:

1. The higher the security level of the facility, the more respect and sometimes even the higher pay the staff receive due to the real or perceived dangerous nature of the inmate population.
2. Agencies frequently require staff to have experience in medium or maximum security facilities as a prerequisite for promotion to supervisory or management positions.
3. The number of positions in medium and maximum security facilities far outnumber those in minimum security.

The 1978 study showed a major policy shift regarding the hiring of women in male institutions. The main concern was no longer for the safety and competence of the women, but for the male inmates' right to privacy. By 1988, the inmate privacy issue was the reason given for placing limits on women's work assignments in the majority of agencies. While nature of the limitations were documented, the impact of them on the number of women hired or their advancement was beyond the scope of this study. These are issues that should be explored in the future.

All but one of the agencies in the top six rankings had limitations on women's work assignments but still managed to hire a significant percentage of women. Again, the great diversity among correctional agencies across the country and even flexibility and degrees of autonomy within agencies provide many opportunities for interpretation of policies. If an agency or a manager needs the manpower and has the commitment, policies will be narrowly interpreted and women hired. The reverse is also true.

The administrative concern for inmate privacy, which the courts have very narrowly granted, is an issue that should be addressed in all facilities regardless of equal employment opportunity. One of the more damaging aspects of prisons for both inmates and staff is the often dehumanizing nature of inmate processing and safekeeping activities such as delousing, strip searching, body cavity searching, and taking urine samples. Some of the invasive aspects of institutional operations cannot be avoided. However, sensitivity to the fact that inmates are human beings and that treating them as such is not a sign of weakness but is a sensible management approach that can only enhance the operation of the facility. Providing privacy screens and other facility modifications, as well as training staff to handle sensitive matters professionally, will only improve the environment for all concerned and help erase the stigma of a "jungle atmosphere" that still haunts some facilities. Taking actions to modify the physical plant and professionalize the officer force will go a long way toward resolving the problems of scheduling staff to man posts. Analyzing security policies and practices concerning the safety and security of the staff members, whether they are male or female, can also only enhance facility operations.

Harassment of female officers by male staff and inappropriate conduct between male inmates and female staff are also issues that should be addressed through positive staff supervision and training. Sexual harassment, in addition to being illegal, wastes valuable staff time and energy. Inappropriate relations between staff and inmates can have a serious impact on institutional operation and security and may be reduced by positively addressing problems of harassment and ostracism of female officers by male staff. It was encouraging that almost half the agencies reported they provided specialized training for women working in male facilities. The nature of that training and an evaluation of its effectiveness should be explored in future studies.

The benefits of hiring women as seen by the agencies appear to support the concept that a heterogeneous work force enriches and improves institutional operations. However, heterogeneous work forces require creative management to maximize the benefits of diversity. Flexibility and the willingness to explore alternative ways of accomplishing the mission of correctional institutions will be a key to the full integration of women into the correctional officer work force. It is encouraging that the majority of agencies are predicting they will continue to expand the number of women they hire into officer positions in male facilities and that women will move up in the organizational ranks. Maintaining the status quo under such circumstances will be impossible. Creative, effective management will be necessary to ensure that agencies make the most of their opportunities to maximize the skills and contributions of all their work force.

References

American Correctional Association. 1981. *Women in corrections* (Monograph, series 1, number 1). College Park, Md.: ACA.

American Correctional Association. 1989. *Juvenile and adult correctional departments, institutions, agencies and paroling authorities*. Laurel, Md.: ACA.

Camp, G. M., & C. G. Camp. 1990. *The correctional yearbook 1990*. South Salem, N.Y.: Criminal Justice Institute.

Chapman, J. 1983. *Women employed in corrections*. Washington, D.C.: National Institute of Justice.

Joint Commission on Correctional Manpower and Training. 1969. *A time to act*. Washington, D.C.: Joint Commission on Correctional Manpower and Training.

U.S. Department of Labor. 1989. *Handbook of labor statistics*. Washington, D.C.: Government Printing Office.

Pregnancy and Correctional Employment

Joann B. Morton, D.P.A.

"What do you women want?" bellowed a corrections administrator in the mid-1970s. "I promoted one of you and then she tells me she's pregnant!" The woman in question performed her management duties in a male medium security institution admirably until the day before she delivered and then returned to work four weeks later. Women employees in corrections had been becoming mothers for years presumably unnoticed, but with the expansion of jobs in male facilities pregnancy came to be viewed as an almost terminal condition. This chapter briefly reviews the background of protective legislation, equal employment, and court rulings, as well as results of an analysis of correctional agency policies concerning pregnancy.

Protective Legislation and Policies

Protective laws, policies, and practices are those established to shelter or guard individuals or a particular group of persons. Protective legislation for the workplace was initially passed during the late 1800s and early 1900s as a part of the overall social reform movement. During the early stages of the Industrial Revolution, women and children were considered an expendable source of cheap labor. African-American women in particular were placed in the dirtiest, most dangerous jobs (Foner 1980). Health and welfare programs for women and children were nonexistent. As Brown (1987, 52) points out, ". . . in 1918, the United States stood eleventh among nations in infant mortality and seventeenth in maternal mortality."

Following the 1920 ratification of the Nineteenth Amendment giving women the right to vote, the coalition of women's groups began to split over the issue of protective legislation (Foner 1980). Some groups argued that the legislation was needed " . . . because women's hours as a rule are longer than men's, women's wages as a rule are lower than men's. Women's economic need is therefore greater than men's" (Foner 1980, 141). The Women's Joint Congressional Committee was formed in 1920 and became an extremely powerful and influential lobby for "protection of women in industry" (Brown 1987, 52). On the other hand, many argued that protective legislation would become another excuse to limit employment opportunities for women.

Proponents of protective legislation for women were successful. Unfortunately, both protective legislation and rules to protect families and children resulted in women being fired to make way for men returning from World War II (Foner 1980). By the time Title VII of the Equal Rights Act passed in 1965, more than half of the states had some form of protective laws for women (Maschke 1989). These usually limited not only the jobs women could hold but also the pay they could receive. In more extreme cases, for example, women could be barmaids but not bartenders—a position which, incidentally, paid more. Although they could work on assembly lines, job rules limited the amount of weight they could lift, so they were paid less than men.

The Equal Employment Opportunity Commission, which was responsible for enforcing Title VII, initially agreed with the concept of protective legislation and different work rules, as did the U. S. Supreme Court. *Geduldig v. Aiello* in 1974 and *General Electric v. Gilbert* in 1976 held that excluding pregnancy benefits from employee insurance policies was not discriminatory.

The Pregnancy Discrimination Act

Responding to public outrage following the Supreme Court decisions on discriminatory benefits, Congress passed the Pregnancy Discrimination Act (PDA) in 1978. This specified the following:

1. A written or unwritten employment policy or practice that excludes from employment opportunities applicants or employees because of pregnancy, childbirth, or related medical conditions is a prima facia violation of Title VII.

2. Disabilities caused or contributed to by pregnancy, childbirth, or related medical conditions, for all job-related purposes, shall be treated the same as disabilities caused or contributed to by other medical conditions, under any health or disability insurance or sick leave plan available in connection with employment. . . . (Pregnancy Discrimination Act 1978, P.L. 95-55J)

41

In 1979, the Equal Employment Opportunity Commission issued guidelines relating to pregnancy, which included the following:

1. Employment policies or practices that exclude pregnant applicants or employees are violations of Title VII.
2. Pregnancy and related disabilities should be treated the same as other medical disabilities in all aspects including amount of leave, accrual of seniority and other benefits, reinstatement, etc., excluding abortion unless medically required if the organization chooses.
3. Any fringe benefit including insurance can in no way treat differently employees affected by pregnancy or related medical conditions.

The issues of pregnancy and work are not insignificant. In 1987, it was estimated that 85 percent of the over 55 million women in the workplace were likely to become pregnant at some time during their employment (Jacobson 1988). Nor did the passage of the Pregnancy Discrimination Act resolve the problems of employers and women workers as demonstrated by the arguments in *U. A. W. v. Johnson Controls, Inc.* In this 1991 case, the employer limited all women, except those whose infertility was medically documented, from jobs involving actual or potential lead exposure that exceeded Occupational Safety and Health Administration Standards. The Supreme Court reversed the lower courts, which had agreed with the employer and held that (1) the employer's policy was facially discriminatory, and (2) the employer did not establish that sex was a bona fide occupational qualification (BFOQ) (*U. A. W. v. Johnson Controls, Inc.* 111 S. Ct. 1196).

While the decision was favorable in terms of banning the limiting of employment opportunities for women of child-bearing age, it was not all-exclusive as it related to the health and safety of all workers in hazardous occupations. Nor did it appear to affirm a woman's rights to choose what might be a dangerous occupation if she were pregnant. Caplan-Cotenoff (1987) argued that the response of states and the private sector to pregnancy discrimination in employment has been inadequate; despite the advantages achieved, more comprehensive action is needed to protect women's rights.

Pregnancy and Corrections

The issue of women as correctional employees gained prominence as women began to enter positions in male institutions. In *Dothard v. Rawlinson* (1977), Justice Stewart wrote: "The (female) employee's very womanhood would thus directly undermine her capacity to provide the security that is the essence of the correctional counselor's responsibility" *(Dothard v. Rawlinson,* 433 U.S. 321, 334, 1977, p. 2730). Zimmer (1986) described prison work environments as characterized by "periodic episodes of extreme violence, constant disruption, turmoil, [and] confusion" (p. 3). However, Flynn noted that evidence indicated that women were a positive influence in institutions and cited a decision of the California Supreme Court that ruled "women must be permitted to take their chances along with men where they are otherwise qualified and capable of meeting the requirements of their employment" (Rafter & Stanko 1982, 328).

National accreditation standards promulgated by the American Correctional Association (1981) contained in the personnel standards the requirement for the inclusion of specific maternity leaves in institution policies, with mandatory leave being at the policy makers' discretion. In regard to pregnant correctional officers, Watson (1990) suggests the following possible arguments for requiring mandatory leave: (1) protection of the fetus in case the mother was physically assaulted and (2) less propensity for self-protection in advanced stages of pregnancy and protection of coworkers. However, others believe the issue of leave should be between the woman and her physician, as it usually is for other temporary disabilities.

Survey Findings

In order to determine the practices common in correctional institutions, a national survey of adult state level correctional agencies was conducted. Questionnaires were sent to adult institutional agencies in all fifty states and the Federal Bureau of Prisons (FBP). Only five states chose not to participate: Maryland, New Jersey, New Mexico, South Dakota, and Wyoming. Questions addressed the issue of written policies pertaining to maternity/paternity leave, and it was requested that copies of them be returned with the survey.

The problem of terminology should be considered when comparing state policies. The term "maternity leave" is generally regarded as prenatal and post-natal leave for new mothers but is not limited to that definition (O'Brien & Madek 1989, 322). Additionally, this analysis was limited to written policies subject to individual interpretations. It must also be recognized that different unwritten policies and practices might exist on-site. The survey was limited to only state adult prison systems and the Federal Bureau of Prisons, thus excluding all other components of corrections at the federal, state, or local level. Results of the survey are summarized in Table 1.

Of the forty-six returned questionnaires, ten agencies (22 percent) indicated having no written policy for maternity/paternity leave. In seven of those agencies, pregnancy was treated as any other disability for which sick leave could be used; one agency normally allowed three months with a doctor's certificate; another adhered to civil service guidelines, which were applicable to all of that state's agencies.

Rhode Island was the only state that differentiated treatment of maternity leave between male and female facilities. In male institutions, pregnancy leave was treated on a case-by-case basis; women's institutions were governed by state personnel rules.

Twenty-five (69 percent) of the thirty-six departments with written maternity policy directives treated maternity leave as sick/temporary disability leave. Five (14 percent) departments noted they had written policies but gave no description of how maternity was treated. Three departments (8 percent) treated it as a leave of absence, giving no indication of whether it was paid or unpaid, while another two (6 percent) treated it as a leave of absence without pay. One (3 percent) department designated that maternity leave be treated as vacation leave.

Of the twenty-five departments denoting maternity leave as sick/temporary disability leave, the time allowed for leave was distributed as follows:

- as much time as needed—one (4 percent) department
- up to one year—three (12 percent) departments
- six months to one year—one (4 percent) department
- seven months—one (4 percent) department
- six months—four (16 percent) departments
- three months—two (8 percent) departments
- nine weeks—one (4 percent) department
- two months—one (4 percent) department

Eight (32 percent) departments did not address the amount of time permitted.

Of the thirty-six departments with written policies, sixteen (44 percent) gave an employee the option to use accrued annual leave or leave without pay as an alternative to sick leave, or in conjunction with sick leave. Only six (17 percent) of the departments chose to include abortion under maternity leave without it being medically required. Paternity leave was allowed by fourteen (39 percent) of the departments. Fourteen of the departments provided for reinstatement of those employees taking maternity leave to their former jobs or one of equal status, as long as policy guidelines were followed.

Conclusions

As Flynn noted, "The road toward equality is fraught with problems" (Rafter & Stanko 1982, 334).The issue of pregnancy requires creativity if the contributions of female correctional employees are to be maximized. It is encouraging that over three-fourths of the state correctional agencies reported having policies relative to pregnancy and maternity leave.

Whether policies are followed is another matter. The United States Navy found in one study of the issue that "male supervisors are largely unfamiliar with policies on pregnancy, and their requirements to counsel pregnant women on their obligations, options, and medical benefits is complied with only about 50 percent of the time" (Barkalow 1990, 244). Additional study is needed to determine whether correctional agencies do in fact follow their policies and whether supervisors and women are aware of their rights.

Ten states reported having no written policies on pregnancy/maternity leave, and conditions varied greatly in those that did. Only fourteen states provided for reinstatement of their employees to former jobs or ones of equal status. These are all causes for considerable concern. They indicate that there is a tendency on the part of some government agencies to ignore not only federal law and professional standards, but more importantly the needs of women employees. Also, the lack of paternity leave provisions has implications for male employees relative to their family responsibilities. These matters raise the question of whether a national parental leave policy as advocated by Caplan-Cotenoff (1987) would improve the situation. It is certainly a matter worth exploring since existing federal legislation and other guidelines appear inadequate.

In practice, the problem of scheduling leave for any type of disability is viewed negatively. One warden noted recently that she handled supervisors' complaints by pointing out that at least with pregnancy they could plan leave and scheduling matters with more certainty than they could with other illnesses or disabling conditions. Supervisors have complained that some pregnant women "use" their condition to avoid less desirable work. However, one supervisor commented somewhat facetiously that this might not be all bad since many women officers were overachievers. As with any group of people, there will always be a few employees who use a situation to what they see as their advantage, as well as some supervisors who may be uncomfortable dealing with the issue realistically. Fortunately, they are in the minority, and most supervisors indicated that pregnant women were overly conscientious in performing their duties.

Just as the issues of protectionism and equal employment have not been resolved in the larger community, questions still remain in corrections. While some aspects of corrections work are unique and may involve potentially dangerous situations, generally there is considerable flexibility in assignment and duties, which enables the effective use of employees whether pregnant or not. However, policies and procedures should ensure that women are not faced with an either/or situation. That is, they should not have to choose between having a family and a career. Women are too vital a resource to have their work contributions limited because of pregnancy/maternity leave, child care, and other family matters. Ideally, correctional employers and employees will work in concert to ensure that all needs are met both for the agency and the workers.

References

American Correctional Association. 1981. *Standards for adult correctional institutions*, 2d. ed. College Park, Md.: ACA.

Barkalow, C.1990. *In the men's house.* New York: Poseidon Press.

Brown, D. M. 1987. *Setting a course, American women in the 1920s.* Boston: Twayne Publishers.

Caplan-Cotenoff, S. A. 1987. Parental leave: The need for a national policy to foster sexual equality. *American Journal of Law and Medicine,* 13: 71-104.

Equal Employment Opportunity Act of 1972, P.L. 92-261 (1972).

Equal Employment Opportunity Commission Compliance Manual, Vol. 2. 1979. Los Angeles: Prentice Hall.

Foner, P. S. 1980.*Women and the American labor movement from World War I to the present.* New York: The Free Press.

Geduldig v. Aiello, 417 U.S. 484 (1974).

General Electric Company v. Gilbert, 429 U.S. 125, 97 S.Ct. 401, 50 L.Ed.2d. 343 (1976).

Jacobson, M. 1988. Pregnancy and employment: Three approaches to equal opportunity. *Boston University Law Review* 68: 1019-1045.

Maschke, K. J. 1989. *Litigation, courts, and women workers.* New York: Praeger.

O'Brien, C. N., & G. A. Madek. 1989. Pregnancy discrimination and maternity leave laws. *Dickinson Law Review* 93: 311-337.

Player, M. A. 1984. *Employment discrimination law: Cases and materials.,* 2nd. ed. St. Paul: West.

Pregnancy Discrimination Act of 1978, P. L. 95-555 (1978).

Rafter, N. H., & E. A. Stanko. 1982. *Judge,lawyer, victim, thief.* Boston: Northeastern University.

Title VII of the Civil Rights Act of 1964, 42 U.S.C. Sec.2000e (1963).

Watson, P. S. 1990. *Duty relief and pregnancy leave for police officers: A national survey.*Unpublished manuscript. University of South Carolina, College of Criminal Justice, Columbia.

Zimmer, L. E. 1986. *Women guarding men.* Chicago: University of Chicago Press.

Table 1
Maternity Leave Policies of Correctional Departments

State	Written Policy		Treatment of Maternity Leave		
	Yes	No	Sick or Disability	Other	No Indication
Alabama	*		*		
Alaska	*				*
Arizona	*		*		
Arkansas	*		*		
California	*			*	
Colorado	*				*
Connecticut	*		*		
Delaware	*		*		
Florida	*		*		
Georgia		*			
Hawaii	*		*		
Idaho	*				*
Illinois	*		*		
Indiana	*		*		

State	Written Policy		Treatment of Maternity Leave		
	Yes	No	Sick or Disability	Other	No Indication
Iowa	*				*
Kansas	*		*		
Kentucky		*			
Louisiana		*			
Maine	*		*		
Massachusetts	*		*		
Michigan	*			*	
Minnesota	*			*	
Mississippi	*				*
Missouri	*		*		
Montana	*		*		
Nebraska		*			
Nevada	*		*		
New Hampshire	*		*		
New York	*		*		
North Carolina	*		*		
North Dakota	*		*		

Table 1—continued

State	Written Policy		Treatment of Maternity Leave		
	Yes	No	Sick or Disability	Other	No Indication
Ohio		*			
Oklahoma	*		*		
Oregon	*			*	
Pennsylvania	*		*		
Rhode Island		*			
South Carolina	*		*		
Tennessee	*		*		
Texas		*			
Utah		*			
Vermont		*			
Virginia		*			
Washington	*			*	
West Virginia	*		*		
Wisconsin	*			*	
FBP, D.C.	*		*		

50

Sexual Harassment

Barbara Jones

When you suspect an employee of bringing contraband into the institution, what is your response? Do you wait until you have clear, objective evidence before you report it or have it investigated? Do you wait until you actually see the staff member bring contraband into the institution before you report it? More likely than not, you bring the information to someone's attention so that an immediate investigation can be conducted. All correctional employees know that bringing contraband into a penal facility is an extremely serious matter that jeopardizes the safety of all staff and the inmate population, creating a dangerous work environment. Thus, immediate action is appropriate once such conduct is suspected.

Does the same immediate response occur when allegations of sexual harassment are made against a staff member? If the answer is no, then as a corrections professional you have failed to realize the serious nature of those complaints; sexual harassment in the workplace creates as much harm as the introduction of contraband. In addition, the presence of sexual harassment in the workplace generates as much, or more, liability for the employer and the offending employee as any inmate civil rights suit.

There is no question that corrections professionals have become well educated about their obligations to manage and operate a penal facility in accordance with the United States Constitution as explained by the respective federal court opinions. There is no doubt that corrections professionals are very much attuned to the law as it relates to the management of the inmate population. The case law today is generally not filled with the sweeping systemwide condition suits that were prevalent in the 1970s and 1980s, reflecting instead unique and individual problems and circumstances. Unfortunately, this painful and expensive education process regarding inmate constitutional rights did not carry over to correctional employees and their work environment.

Admittedly, the physical environment of penal facilities has improved because of renovation and/or construction that occurred in response to federal court orders or settlements.

Training for all staff levels has also improved the quality of the work environment for correctional employees. Women have been hired in many nontraditional positions in penal facilities—albeit reluctantly in some states (*Griffin v. Michigan Department of Corrections*). Unfortunately, the attitude of a formerly male-dominated profession has not changed as dramatically toward female employees as it has changed toward inmates. Many women working in penal facilities are working in a hostile environment as a result of sometimes deliberate, often subtle, and mostly unintentional sexual harassment. Certainly male staff can be sexually harassed, and sexual harassment can occur between members of the same sex. However, the majority of sexual harassment complaints involve women harassed by their male co-workers or supervisors. Subjecting any employee to such a work environment is against the law (*Meritor Savings Bank v. Vinson*).

Liability

Sexual harassment can impose as serious a liability on the employer and offending employee as the liability imposed when an inmate is found to have been treated in an unconstitutional manner. The implementation of simple and effective measures in the workplace can quickly improve the work environment as well as reduce potential liability. A formula for a good professional work environment can be put in place by developing and implementing appropriate policies.

Sexual harassment of an employee violates federal law (Title VII) and can also be a violation of the Federal Civil Rights Act through the First Amendment (*Connick v. Myers*) (retaliatory discharge for complaining) or the Equal Protection Clause (*Davis v. Passman; Starrett v. Wadley; Long v. Laramie County Community College Dist.*) (discriminatory conduct occurred solely because of employee's sex). Sexual harassment can be a violation of a state's civil rights act as well as a violation of state tort law (intentional infliction of emotional distress, common-law battery, wrongful discharge). Usually all claims are consolidated in one proceeding. A successful litigant can be awarded actual damages (e.g., back pay, front pay), equitable relief (e.g., reinstatement, change in policies), and damages. In all instances, if the complaining party is successful, attorneys' fees and costs may be awarded. Thus, if a complaining employee can demonstrate that he or she has been subjected to sexual harassment, the employee can receive the same or similar remedies inmates receive when they successfully sue correctional employees for unconstitutional treatment.

Title VII of the United States Code specifies:

> It shall be an unlawful employment practice for an employer . . . to fail or refuse to hire or to discharge any individual, or otherwise to discriminate against any individual with respect to his compensation, terms, conditions, or privileges of employment, because of such individual's race, color, religion, sex, or national origin[.]
> —Section 703(a)(1) of Title VII, 42 U. S. C. S2000(e-2) (a)

Guidelines*

In 1980, The Equal Employment Opportunity Commission (EEOC) issued guidelines that defined the circumstances under which certain conduct could be considered sexual harassment such that an employer and/or an employee could be held liable.

The EEOC has defined sexual harassment as follows:

> Unwelcome sexual advances, requests for sexual favors, and other verbal or physical conduct of a sexual nature constitute sexual harassment when (1) submission to such conduct is made either explicitly or implicitly a term or condition of an individual's employment, (2) submission to or rejection of such conduct by an individual is used as the basis for employment decisions affecting such individual, or (3) such conduct has the purpose or effect of unreasonably interfering with an individual's work performance or creating an intimidating, hostile, or offensive conducting work environment (29 C. F. R. S1604.11).

After reading the federal statute and the guidelines established by the EEOC, no reasonable person would question the common-sense employment purpose of the statute and guidelines. Application of these, however, is a much more difficult task. Much of the unlawful conduct can be very subtle, and in many cases is unintentional. Often the offense occurs outside the presence of witnesses. None of those factors makes the conduct any less serious; it just makes an investigation more difficult.

For an in-depth review of the Commission guidelines as applied by the Commission and various federal courts, see EEOC Policy Statement N 915-050, issued March 19, 1990.

Every effort should be made by the employer to stop any form of sexual harassment in the workplace. The law prohibits offensive and unwelcome conduct of a sexual nature. Complaints of sexual harassment by any employee are entitled to an immediate response, which should include at minimum some type of investigation. When conducting a preliminary investigation, the question is not whether the offending person intended to offend or harass an employee; the question is whether conduct occurred that was unwelcome, offensive, and of a sexual nature as viewed by the complaining employee. If the conduct did occur and adversely affects the employee's ability to perform his or her job, and if the employer knew or should have known of the harassment and failed to take appropriate action, sexual harassment resulting in a hostile work environment will be found to exist (*Ramsey v. City and County of Denver; Drinkwater v. Union Carbide Corp.; Steele v. Offshore Shipbuilding, Inc.; Staton v. Maries County*).

The most obvious form of sexual harassment is conduct described as *quid pro quo*, where submission to sexual advances is a condition of employment. Surely, no employer would question that this type of conduct is totally inappropriate and should be unlawful. Requiring an employee to submit to sexual advances as a condition of getting a job, remaining on the job, or being promoted is unlawful; in all instances an employer will be held strictly liable for that conduct, whether or not the employer had any knowledge of the conduct.

The more difficult situation for an employer is when an employee complains about a coworker or supervisor who is behaving in an unwelcome, offensive, and sexual nature such that a hostile, abusive work environment exists. In many instances this conduct may take place in a private setting on the job site, away from witnesses. This type of conduct could include offensive language, touching, and inappropriate and suggestive comments focused on the sex of the complaining employee.

Unwelcome and offensive conduct of a sexual nature can also occur in a group setting, such as in staff meetings where inappropriate comments of a sexual nature are made to a group by a coworker or supervisor. Sometimes this conduct may not appear to offend; most employees would rather go along with the group than object to inappropriate, unwelcome, and offensive comments or conduct. The offending party usually responds to complaints by stating, "Oh, I didn't mean anything," "I was just kidding around," or "It was nothing personal. I would never sexually harass anyone."

54

The impact on the complaining employee is the focus, not the intent of the offending party. However, intent may later play a role if damages are sought. Unwelcome verbal or physical conduct of a sexual nature that is offensive to an employee and unreasonably interferes with an employee's work performance creates an intimidating, abusive work environment and may be subject to action under federal and state law.

Types of Liability

Depending on the type of sexual harassment that is found to have occurred, *quid pro quo* or a hostile work environment, the liability of the employer differs. Generally, an employer is held strictly liable for any *quid pro quo* sexual harassment, whether the employer knew or should have known of the situation. In some instances, if the hostile work environment is so severe that an employer knew or should have known about it, then an employer can also be held strictly liable. However, in the hostile work environment situation it is generally the offending employee who is held personally liable.

An employer can avoid liability for sexual harassment by responding promptly and effectively (*Guess v. Bethlehem; Rabidue v. Osceola Refining Co.; Barrett v. Omaha National Bank; Katz v. Dole*). Generally, a single act of inappropriate conduct is not sufficient to establish sexual harassment. Thus, if an employer responds to a complaint of sexual harassment and makes every effort to stop it, there should be no liability for the employer.

Circumstantial evidence will support a claim for sexual harassment because it is recognized that unlawful conduct does not usually occur in front of witnesses. In most sexual harassment cases, the complaining employee is embarrassed and has a difficult time coming forward. This is especially true if sexual favors were demanded and received as a condition of the employment, or if the sexual relationship was initially consensual and was later terminated. In many instances, an employee fears retaliation for complaining about sexual harassment and believes the serious nature of the problem will not be appreciated. Administrators and supervisors can eliminate this concern by making it clear to all staff that such complaints are welcome, will be treated with respect, and will be responded to in an appropriate manner.

Many factors should be considered when an employer receives a complaint of sexual harassment, whether it be *quid pro quo* or a hostile work environment situation. One factor that is generally helpful is determining whether the complaining employee attempted to stop the offensive conduct at an early stage, either by complaining to the offending party, to a personal friend, a coworker, a supervisor, or through a formal complaint using the employer's grievance procedure. If some action has been taken at an early stage by the complaining employee, it aids in assessing that employee's credibility, especially when other witnesses are unavailable to support the charge. An employer should check with an employee's friends at work or outside work to determine if he or she has discussed the problem with them. This is not to say that a failure of the employee to discuss the problem is evidence that he or she was not harassed, but it is a factor that may aid the investigation.

Sometimes the investigation may be brief, and the problem may be resolved quickly by confronting the offending employee to determine whether the conduct has occurred and, if it has, advising the employee of the consequence if such conduct does not cease. Sometimes it may be necessary to separate the offending employee and the offended employee at work. In this situation, one must make certain that the offended employee is not subjected to a penalization through the separation.

Steps to Avoid Sexual Harassment

If the employer has an effective complaint procedure and encourages complaints for appropriate resolution, liability can be reduced. Implementing effective training programs on sexual harassment for all staff on a routine basis will also improve the work environment. Most corrections departments today have a mechanism in place, through written policies and procedures, to have relevant and effective training on sexual harassment and a grievance procedure for employees.

Several other steps can be taken by an employer to avoid the potential for sexual harassment in the workplace. First, as an administrator or supervisor, conduct a personal examination of your management style. Acquaint yourself with the law, treat sexual harassment complaints seriously, and personally communicate this attitude of intolerance to your management staff and your line staff in meetings. Establish a viable grievance procedure and maintain an open-door policy for complaints, either through a formalized grievance procedure or informally. Determine whether you are a person who communicates through touching. Touching can be offensive to others and, although not intended as such, it can be viewed as sexual harassment.

You should also determine whether you express yourself with language that may be considered inappropriate, unwelcome, or of a sexual nature. Use of such language should cease immediately. Although you may not use such language with an intent to harass, it can create a hostile work environment and may be considered, in certain circumstances, unlawful.

A personal examination by every employee should be conducted to determine whether there are personal characteristics that may be viewed as offensive to others, and such conduct should cease. This self-examination should be part of an orientation to all staff in order to make employees aware not only of their own personal habits, but also aware of what conduct will not be tolerated in the work environment.

If you have observed any inappropriate conduct toward a coworker, you should report it immediately to a supervisor or an EEOC officer so that the conduct can be stopped. An educated, responsive, and well-trained Equal Employment Opportunity officer should be in place at each institution and in central office where applicable. Evaluate the appointment of your EEOC officer and determine whether he or she is a "token" appointment or whether that position is crucial to the successful operation of your organization.

Because of the very nature of correctional facilities, the military model works well to operate and maintain a secure institution. The chain of command is always paramount. However, this "chain of command" attitude sometimes gets in the way of effectively handling employee complaints and problems. Because a rigid complaint procedure discourages complaints, an administrator should not insist that an employee with a complaint follow the chain of command or the formalized grievance procedure and no other. If there is no reasonable alternative for an employee to communicate complaints other than through the chain, as an administrator you have not provided an open door or flexible policy to receive complaints. It should be clear to all employees that if they have a more comfortable way of voicing their complaints, such a method is acceptable. Remember that an employer must promptly and effectively respond to sexual harassment complaints when brought to the employer's attention or when the employer should have known of the problem.

Finally, conduct an inspection similar to a security inspection or a program inspection to determine whether offensive visuals—such as sexually explicit calendars, postcards, or jokes—are posted in work areas. These types of materials should be removed from all work stations.

All staff should enforce appropriate conduct between in-mates and staff of the same or opposite sex. Any inappropriate, offensive, and unwelcome sexual conduct by an inmate toward any staff should be treated as a violation of institutional rules, and appropriate disciplinary measures should be taken.

Corrections has come a long way in re-educating employees to the operation of their facilities. We need to improve the operation even more, so that our valuable employees are working in a positive, responsive, and professional environment. Correctional employees are held to a very high standard of care toward inmates; that same high standard should be applied toward each other.

Court Cases

Barrett v. Omaha National Bank 726 F.2d 424 (8th Cir. 1984)

Connick v. Myers 461 U.S. 138, 103 S.Ct. 1684, 75 L.Ed. 2d 708 (1983)

Davis v. Passman 442 U.S. 228, 99 S.Ct. 2264 60 L.Ed. 2d 846 (1979)

Drinkwater v. Union Carbide Corporation 904 F.2d 843 (3rd Cir. 1990)

Griffin v. Michigan Department of Corrections 654 F. Supp. 690 (E.D. Mich. 1982)

Guess v. Bethlehem Steel Corporation 913 F.2d 473 (7th Cir. 1990)

Katz v. Dole 709 F.2d 251 (4th Cir. 1983)

Long v. Laramie County Community College District 804 F.2d 743 (10th Cir. 1988) cert. den'd 488 U.S. 824, 109 S.Ct. 73, 102 L.Ed. 2d 50 (1988)

Meritor Savings Bank v. Vinson 477 U.S. 57, 106 S.Ct. 2399, 91 L.Ed. 49 (1986)

Rabidue v. Osceola Refining Company 805 F.2d 611 (6th Cir 1986) cert. den'd 481 U.S. 1941, 107 S.Ct. 1983, 95 L.Ed. 2d 823 (1987)

Ramsey v. City and County of Denver 907 F.2d 1004 (10th Cir. 1990)

Starrett v. Wadley 876 F.2d 808 (10th Cir. 1989)

Staton v. Maries County 868 F.2d 996 (8th Cir. 1989)

Steele v. Offshore Shipbuilding, Incorporated 867 F.2d 1311 (11th Cir. 1989)

Coping Strategies For Women In All-male Correctional Facilities

Rose Etheridge, Cynthia Hale,
and Margaret Hambrick

There are certain pitfalls for women who are working in all-male correctional facilities. Taking certain steps and having a firm knowledge of effective procedures will help avoid these pitfalls.

Women can take concrete steps to keep from falling victim to stereotypical images. The first step is careful and extensive self-examination. Plato's admonition to "know thyself" will likely never be more important than now as women in corrections attempt to overcome the attitudinal barriers to their full acceptance in all-male settings. Women must examine their own attitudes and motivations for working in corrections, clearly establishing who they are and what they want to do. Once this important initial step is taken, they can then begin to build the kind of image they will need to carry out their jobs safely and competently. The following are specific coping techniques for female correctional staff in all-male settings:

Interact with inmates in a straightforward, nonmanipulative manner and do so consistently. As one inmate in an all-male facility put it: "It's not that the women here ain't about business. It's just that some of them ain't about business all the time." The lesson here for the female correctional worker is not to contaminate the image she is trying to convey by being inconsistent. Inconsistent interactions or a lack of congruence between verbal and nonverbal messages is confusing and difficult to interpret. She must know the message she wants to convey and do so clearly and matter-of-factly.

One of the most difficult tasks for a new woman employee is walking across the compound. She feels hundreds of eyes on her. If she hurries across trying not to see anyone or if she seems to relish the attention and moves her body in response,

This chapter was exempted with permission from "Female Employees in All-male Correctional Facilities" in the December 1985 issue of Federal Probation.

she has lost professional status. In this instance, as always, she should walk purposefully and with deliberate speed: Walk with head erect. Make eye contact. Extend a greeting in a business-like manner.

The female correctional officer is likely to receive compliments, especially at first, and how she responds gives the inmates clues. The best response is a clipped "thank you" or a nod and a quick movement to a more business-like topic. She has acknowledged that she is the opposite sex, while indicating that her purpose is business.

Develop a reputation for treating inmates fairly and impartially. The female correctional worker must not single out certain inmates for special favors and privileges. Also, she must be aware of how she is spending her time and who she is spending it with. Inmates, by virtue of their position, are keen observers of the subtleties operating in the correctional environment. They know if a woman staff member is spending a disproportionate amount of time with a particular inmate. Once the message gets around (and news travels fast in a prison), the woman in question has developed a reputation for showing partiality and favoritism. When this happens, a challenge to her authority or a bid for her favors is usually just around the corner.

Dress appropriately. Some authorities have identified certain ways of dressing that produce images that either help or hinder a woman's job performance. The prison environment, with its usually limited numbers of women, exacerbates the problems that can occur over the issue of dress. The clothes women wear send a message. Both staff and inmates will be looking at how the female employee dresses to find clues to how she feels about herself and how she is going to act toward them. Dress that is either too feminine or too masculine will cause problems.

Dressing in a very feminine or sexy fashion will be interpreted as a signal of the employee's availability, and she will probably be approached on that basis. A rejection or denial will also cause problems because the physical cues will contradict what she is verbalizing. This can be taken as saying no when meaning yes. Low-cut necklines, see-through clothes, and short or slit skirts are inappropriate in any professional work environment and especially so in a prison. Given that a very feminine style can cause problems, the female correctional worker may be tempted to go to the other extreme and dress in a very masculine manner. This too creates some problems, although perhaps more with other staff than with inmates. Masculine dress can and will be interpreted as an indicator of sexual deviance. This also reinforces the old stereotype that only women who want to be men are interested in working in corrections.

The clothing guide for work in a prison environment is much the same as dressing for any professional position. If there is a uniform required, wear it well. Make sure that it is properly fitted and sized. If it is designed only for men, or if the women's version does not have the conveniences required, such as pockets or belt loops, complain through proper channels. The uniform should be clean and pressed, and the employee must resist the impulse to feminize it by adding to it.

If there is no uniform required for a particular position, personal dress should be conservative. The clothing should fit well. Skirts and jackets are preferred, and the skirts should reach just below the knee. Blouses should not be sheer. They should be tailored and not frilly. In short, while on the job, a professional, no-nonsense image should be projected. There should be no dichotomy between how the female employee dresses and what she is required to do.

Be prepared for initial negative reactions. Anything new in a prison setting is potential threat, and the introduction of women to the staff in an all-male facility is no exception. Accept the fact that at first no one knows you well enough to have a personal grudge against you. Rather, any initial negative reaction is probably a reaction to what you represent (e.g., change, authority). Recognize that physical traits such as age, race, height, and weight may cause inmates or staff to react to you in a particular way regardless of what you say or do. Tearing down expectations based on stereotypical images may take time, but it is worth the investment.

Maintain a professional distance from inmates. Don't get too involved in their personal lives and dealings on the compound. A role of professionalism allows for the kind of objectivity that makes for sound decisions and prevents the emotional drain that ends in burnout. The professional role may be hard to maintain because of the pressure from inmates to be more "personal." As one inmate expressed it:

"Nurses are hard to talk to because they're always taking notes when they're talking, like an intern. I want more personal conversation. It's like they're professional, like they really didn't take in all you're saying when they're writing."

The professional role need not be synonymous with coldness and impersonality, although to the lonely inmate who wants female companionship the professional role may seem distant indeed.

Deal with conflict decisively and assertively. Don't be afraid of confrontation. On the other hand, don't hesitate to use other approaches when appropriate. Know the difference between being assertive and being aggressive. As a rule, "assertive" opens doors that "aggressive" can't.

Build positive relationships with male coworkers. Even though you may be met with a less than enthusiastic reception, treat male coworkers cordially and professionally at all times. Inmates often take their cue as to how to relate to female staff from observing what male staff say about a particular woman and how they relate to her. Although a woman can't control vicious, unprovoked rumors started by men threatened by her presence, she can keep from adding fuel to the fire. Inmates are very observant and can quickly weed out false pieces of information simply by observing disparities between a woman's behavior and what is said about her.

Develop a support network of other women in the organization. The support of other women in the organization can be a key source of comfort and fortification in stressful times. Women who have been on the job for a while can offer guidance and advice from the wisdom their experience has provided. New employees can help each other by sharing their experiences and perceptions, letting each other know that "you're not in this alone."

It may even be helpful to create a formal organization of female correctional employees to deal more formally and in-depth with the career issues of women. Care must be taken, however, not to become cliquish and exclusive. Special interest groups have a way of developing into factions, and factions can quickly create divisiveness and become isolated from the mainstream of the prison environment. If a formal organization seems to meet a need, go ahead with it, but invite men to the meetings. Make an effort to sensitize them to the concerns of women in correctional settings.

Keep an open mind. Try to avoid snap judgements, and look at all sides of issues. Think of your job as one of information-gatherer in addition to your formal duties. Develop an inquiring mind and work to develop creative solutions to problems.

Your very survival in the organization may depend on this ability.

Be supportive of other women. People judge a woman by what she says about other women. Women who criticize other women are considered insecure and vulnerable. The woman who criticizes other women hurts herself and other women as well. A woman will face enough roadblocks on the job without having more erected by those who share her ordeal.

Do your job. Neither ask for nor accept special favors. Don't let others make allowances for you because you're a woman. Show by your actions that your femaleness will not be a burden to fellow staff and inmates. Never use your femaleness as an excuse.

Prepare for the next job. Any person looking to move up the career ladder of an organization must be preparing to meet the qualifications at the next step. Potential future jobs should be identified and the requirements for them determined. Learning experiences on the job should be sought even if that means working an undesirable shift or post. If necessary, go back to school during off hours for the required education or specialty training.

Many correctional employers require geographical mobility for promotion, and this can be an extremely difficult question for a woman. She must determine if this is a factor and make her decisions about it. If mobility is required, the woman must be willing to move or accept the fact that however good and qualified she is, she may not be selected for promotion.

Keep your mental health in good repair. Corrections is a highly emotional business. Correctional workers deal with human lives and destinies. Inmates will sap them of emotional strength if they let them. The self-control and situational control needed to do the job is also draining. If the female correctional worker is not an emotionally strong person, corrections is not for her. Even people who are emotionally vulnerable for a specific reason, who normally may be strong, need to be cautious. A sympathetic inmate ear offered to a newly divorced woman can be tempting. The inmate may be able to provide exactly the kind of support needed, but the context is wrong. It is an adage in corrections that "your personal business is no business of inmates."

Women who are not used to male attention can have problems dealing with the sudden deluge they will receive. Keep a perspective and realize that, to male inmates in their state of sexual deprivation, anything resembling a female is attractive. A woman must not be flattered into thinking that she is the most special, attractive, desirable woman that has ever walked through the door. It is difficult to keep from losing perspective in an environment where women may become the objects of adoration. Many women find it helpful to develop a satisfying private life outside the institution. They must not let their work become their only source of reward, fulfillment, and satisfaction. Develop stimulating friendships and interests unrelated to work.

A Woman's Place in Male Corrections

What do women have to offer as members of the staff in all-male institutions? Do women have anything to offer that is distinctly different from their male colleagues? What is a woman's place in male corrections? The answer to the last question is any place and all places.

The presence of women in the work force of all-male institutions is relatively new, particularly in positions men have traditionally filled, such as correctional officer. It is no secret that expectation of women's performance is high, perhaps disproportionately so. There is concern on the part of their male counterparts and inmates as to whether women are capable of performing the duties that are required of correctional personnel. The worry is whether women can handle the physically and mentally demanding and stressful situations that one is confronted with in the correctional setting. Being considered the "weaker sex" could seemingly put women at a disadvantage, if what is expected is brawn as opposed to brains. All correctional personnel are required to show professionalism, competency, and the ability to use their head, both in a crisis and in the performance of day-to-day responsibilities. What is expected of women is no different, and women can offer no less. As Camille Graham, former Deputy Director of Adult Institutions, Arizona Department of Corrections, concludes:

> The only ingredients necessary for being a woman employed in a male institution also apply to male correctional workers. Masculine traits are not necessary—professional traits are (Graham 1981, 27).

Women must conduct themselves in the workplace with the highest degree of professionalism and competence. It is quality job performance that will distinguish women in all-male institutions, as in any organization or career they enter.

Because of undeniable physiological differences and the unique role women occupy in society, female correctional workers do have something distinctly different from men to offer the correctional environment. The male inmate, though for the moment barred from normal contact with women, has developed an image of what a woman is or should be. Unfortunately, the image that many of them have of women is neither positive nor healthy. A woman is, to many of them, an object of pleasure, subordination, or abuse. Inmates tend to hold onto these images of women as the norm and may not be aware or open to the possibility of more positive images. At best, women are viewed as little more than objects—dependent, needing protection, and incapable of being independent career women sharing responsibility with men.

Women employed as correctional staff in all-male institutions can provide inmates with positive images of women. They exercise power and give the inmates an opportunity to observe and interact with them as professionals. Women in positions of authority may cause some immediate discomfort to the inmate while, at the same time, they disrupt his perception of women. Perhaps they will, in some way, induce him to take women seriously and view them—not as objects of pleasure and abuse or as dependent, dumb creatures, or as those to be feared or revered because of some power they may have over him—but rather as persons of integrity, intellect, and ability.

Presenting positive images will depend largely on how a woman conducts herself in the institution. She is highly visible in the correctional community, which observes the way she dresses, the way she walks, and the way she relates to other staff and inmates. When relating to staff and inmates, a woman should be comfortable with herself. She is not a man; she should not act like a man. In fact, coworkers may find it difficult to relate to a woman who masquerades as a man. She is expected to display the warmth, sensitivity, and understanding that are usually attributed to women—traits that all correctional employees would be well-advised to develop and refine. The woman should be feminine but firm, be assertive and not play games. She should make sure that people know where she stands at all times. It is important for her to be honest, forthright, and a person of her word. It is not wise to make promises that she does not intend to or cannot keep. Expectations regarding a woman's performance are high; there is little room for error, especially where matters of personal integrity are concerned.

Single-sex institutions are abnormal settings and make incarceration even more difficult for inmates. The presence of women in all-male institutions brings some normalcy to the situation. Many inmates maintain that the presence of women in the institutions helps them feel like they are still a part of the real world. Others report that they groom themselves more carefully and watch their language, manners, and behavior more diligently in the presence of women (Graham 1981; Petersen 1982). Perhaps the presence of women in all-male prisons is just what is called for to add elements of humaneness and civility to an all-too-often hostile and uncivilized environment.

Conclusion

The struggle of women for the right to work in the male correctional environment in jobs that carry higher salaries and promotion potential seems to be over. However, their struggle to win the acceptance of their male coworkers and male inmates and to achieve the cooperation needed to give them an even chance of succeeding is just beginning.

The woman who finds herself working in a male correctional environment must realistically face the ingrained attitudes of her male (and often female) coworkers and inmates and be prepared to deal with them. This requires a thorough knowledge of what those attitudes are likely to be and ways of coping with them effectively. At the same time, she must maintain her sense of self-worth and contribution to her chosen field.

The removal of the legal and formal barriers to employment has been only the first step. The larger task of removing the less tangible human barriers of the workplace remains. It is vital that, given the small numbers, every woman do her best to succeed. It is only with the continuing progress of women through the ranks of male corrections and into top management that the place of women overall is finally assured.

References

Graham, Camille G. 1981. Women are succeeding in male institutions. In *Women in corrections* (Monograph, series 1, number 1). College Park, Md.: ACA.

Petersen, Cheryl Bowser. 1982. Doing time with the boys: An analysis of women correctional officers in all-male facilities. In *The criminal justice system and women*. Barbara R. Price and Natalie J. Sokoloff, eds. New York: Clark Boardman Co., Ltd.

Managing Success

Helen G. Corrothers

Now, here, you see, it takes all the running you can do, to keep in the same place. If you want to get somewhere else, you must run at least twice as fast as that!

—The Red Queen to Alice in Alice's Adventures in Wonderland & Through the Looking-Glass *by Lewis Carroll.*

Women are now working in all areas of corrections, from line officers in maximum security prisons to wardens, from probation and parole officers to chief probation officers and commissioners of parole and corrections. The contributions of women to the field of corrections are recognized as vital to the effectiveness of every correctional agency. While the war is not over, the number of successful campaigns is sufficient to make relevant concern for managing this success.

The controlling, handling, or managing of success is critical to ensuring its retention. What we think of as success, the difficulty of its attainment, and the relevance of these obstacles to its management will be explored in this chapter. Subsequently, the challenge of juggling professional and personal responsibilities as well as professional burnout, victimization, and stress management will be discussed.

Success

What is success? It is the attainment of one's goals. Goals among individuals differ; success for one person is not necessarily success for another. It has been said that success is getting what you want; happiness is wanting what you get. Opinions vary concerning the goals generally sought by women with careers. One author, discussing the differences between the way men and women view a career in male-dominated businesses, said, "I have never heard a man talk about fulfillment in a career. When I began working with women, I was really surprised to hear the word used frequently." While the author viewed this approach to a career as "healthier" and "more sensible," he thought it to be significantly unique (Tunick 1990). Helen J. McLane (1980) more accurately captures women's aspirations in any field when she writes that women "basically want the same things as men: responsibility, challenge, opportunity for advancement, and appropriate compensation." Concerning advancement, if you still feel excitement and see challenge in your current position, then managing your success may be retaining what you have achieved.

Success has been an elusive quality for women in corrections, and the road to its achievement has been rough. Many of the qualities and attributes that enabled women to acquire an initial measure of success remain vital to the retention and advancement or management of success. The difficulty of the struggle for success places a higher value on its retention. A 1990 report in the *Washington Post* on *The American Woman 1990-91* notes that "a key obstacle to economic security for many women is persistent race and sex discrimination in America's workplaces . . ." Limited opportunities are among the obstacles to successful careers.

A 1969 Joint Commission on Correctional Manpower and Training survey found that women constituted 40 percent of the national work force but only 12 percent of the correctional work force. Most of these women worked in institutions for female offenders. Since the majority of correctional institutions were for male offenders, women's opportunities for advancement and for success were limited. The survey found that when state and federal institutions hired women, they were employed as clerks and secretaries. Because they were not allowed to follow the then-traditional route to promotion or come up through the ranks, successful careers eluded them: they were "effectively eliminated from [consideration for] management and administrative positions" (National Advisory Commission on Criminal Justice Standards and Goals 1975).

The difficulties for women in corrections are not unique. In general society during 1980 it was found that while women's aspirations as managers and leaders were increasing, more than half of all women employed (then 42 percent of the work force) were engaged in clerical or service work. Even when professional careers were realized, women tended to be placed in "nonsupervisory and technical roles, rather than managerial positions that lead to the apex of the corporate pyramid." Psychological and sociological barriers were cited as providing the barriers to the mid- and upper-level management ranks (McLane 1980).

There has been what can be called an attitude barrier. With legal barriers crumbling, public attitudes about the worth and appropriate roles for women become more significant.[1] One of the reasons for the persistent attitudinal problem concerning changing roles for women is the lack of knowledge about women in criminal justice. The coverage of women in criminal justice literature focuses on women offenders and women prisoners. Women offenders have themselves received scant attention compared to male offenders, so much so that they have been termed "the forgotten offenders." It was not until 1979 that research was conducted concerning women correctional officers (Feinman 1980).[2]

Consequently, part of the solution of maintaining the success women have achieved is to increase public awareness, both collectively and individually, of the duties women perform and how well they perform them. Attitudes also constitute a personal challenge in that it is necessary for women to develop enough confidence in their expertise to ensure competence. One author discusses the connection between self-esteem and salary, saying that "the more confidence a woman gains, the easier it is for her to get paid what she's worth" (McGarvey 1988). This factor of attitude cannot be quickly dismissed. If we expect failure, the world will not stand in our way. The necessary ambition, self-discipline, willpower, and ability to work with others are essential.

An additional factor important to success and its retention is setting goals. In *Seeds of Greatness* (1983), Denis Waitley says, "the reason so many individuals fail to achieve their goals in life is that they never really set them in the first place." Knowing yourself and your best qualities are helpful. Lester Korn, a corporate recruiting expert, has said: "People who succeed know what they can do and what they cannot. They know, in sum, who they are. Those who do not succeed haven't a clue" (Korn 1988).

Only by knowing what you ultimately want from life can you do periodic progress checks. In his speech accepting nomination to the nation's highest office, George Bush talked about his personal sense of mission in life. Most successful people—whether or not they would express it this way—sense that they have a mission in life, that they are here to make a difference. Richard Nelson Bolles, a leading career counselor, writes:

The motive that drives us to search for A Sense of Mission is our desire for some reassurance of our Uniqueness. We want to see that we are not just another grain of sand lying on the beach called humanity, out- numbered and lost in the five billion mass, but that the Universe—God—caused us to be born and be put here for some unique reason: to contribute to Life on earth something no one else can contribute in quite the same way. At its very minimum, then, if you search for a sense of Mission you are searching for reassurance that the world is at least a little bit richer for your being here; and a little bit poorer after your going (Bolles 1990).

Effectiveness and efficiency through effort are essential. A belief in luck is out. Someone once said, "I'm a great believer in luck and the harder I work the more I have of it." Vince Lombardi once explained that luck is when preparation meets opportunity.

Set high standards and compete with yourself. It is impor- tant to be the best that you can be. Compete with excellence. Even as the authors of *Megatrends 2000* cheered the prospects for women's future success in the information economy, they indicated the significance of the "one factor holding them

back—themselves" (Naisbitt & Aburdene 1990). They note that women over thirty today formulated their career goals in a different world, and they probably set their goals too low. They cautioned that now "at the dawn of the 1990s, the decade when women's leadership comes of age, it is time that women started reexamining those goals. For many it is time to revise them upward." Women must set their sights toward goals never before planned or dreamed possible. Stretch yourself. Look for challenge and don't forget to compete with yourself. And don't forget to have a sense of humor.

The woman who is successful in her profession must at the same time cope successfully with personal responsibilities, professional burnout, victimization, and stress. Among the personal challenges for most mothers are child care concerns. Both presidential candidates, during the last election, identified child care providers and facilities as national concerns. The percentage of working women with babies less than one year old increased from 32 percent in 1977 to 43 percent five years later to 52 percent by 1987 (McGarvey 1988). In 1991, the National Center for Health Statistics reported approximately 4.1 million live births in the one-year period ending September 30, 1990, representing a 4 percent increase from the previous year. While researchers are not yet able to explain this largest increase in twenty-six years, child care difficulties are more significant because "unlike the boom of the 1950s and 1960s, this wave comes when most mothers are in the work force . . ." (Vobejda 1991).

Additionally, more and more families extend beyond spouse and children. Because Americans are living longer, frequently a parent becomes the responsibility of a child. Numerous articles note that career women are disproportionately represented among the caretakers for elderly parents. (According to the Bureau of National Affairs, Washington, D.C., three-quarters of the caretakers are women and mothers.) It is predicted perhaps optimistically that this problem will be alleviated because elder care programs will flourish. "Human resources and facilities currently devoted to preschool day care eventually would be expanded to include the elderly" (Kent 1990).

A balance between your personal and professional lives is important. Find the balance that feels right for you. It is important to carve out of the family time some purely personal time to alleviate stress.

The American woman is expected to be perfect in all aspects of her life, both personal and professional: she must be

Superwoman. She is told she can have it all, with an implied "you can do it all, and perfectly." We are not superwomen, although the attempt to become so contributes to our level of stress. We are recognizing that we can successfully manage our lives by being less than perfect, subsequently reducing our stress. A Gallup survey of 1,000 working women conducted in December 1987 found that working not only does not seem to undercut family life but has the opposite effect. Three-quarters of working women rated the quality of their family as "very good." Professional career women were more likely than those with blue collar jobs to have this opinion (81 percent compared with 68 percent) (Braiker 1988).

In the past, many women were forced to make a choice between having a career or a family. (The "mommy track" is a modern and less overt method used by firms to limit career advancement.) We should be able to have it all. We should also have the assurance that we need not be superwomen.

Victimization

A little recognized problem that is faced too often by women is victimization. A discussion of this problem is included here because it is a fact of life for many women and can influence success and productivity in the workplace, as well as stress levels. Research on the victimization of women was conducted by the Department of Justice's National Crime Survey Program (NCS) beginning in 1973. Their information indicated a dramatic increase in rape, robbery, and assault against women over a seventeen-year period (Flowers 1977). Statistics show that a woman is raped in the United States once every six minutes, and an estimated 3 to 4 million American women each year are beaten by their husbands or partners (National Woman Abuse Prevention Project 1989). Domestic violence crosses all racial and socioeconomic lines.

Other less dramatic forms of victimization are self-inflicted. With success comes additional demands on our time, more requests for speeches, participation in projects, and other activities. Coupled with a reluctance to say no, these time-intensive activities contribute to a high level of stress.

Stress Management and Professional Burnout

Correctional employees are experiencing professional burnout. "Job burnout is succinctly defined by Maslach and Jackson (1981:99) as 'a syndrome of emotional exhaustion and cynicism that occurs frequently among individuals who do 'people work' of some kind'" (Whitehead & Lindquist 1986).

They describe the job burnout process as producing three conditions: Emotional exhaustion or feelings that you are overextended and exhausted by your job responsibilities; depersonalization that causes impersonal and cynical interactions with clients; and a lack of personal accomplishment. The Maslach Burnout Inventory (MBI) is a widely used survey instrument designed to measure these three components to determine the degree of perceived burnout experienced by personnel in social service fields (Whitehead & Lindquist 1986).

Some researchers (Maslach 1982) believe that burnout results primarily from the stress of dealing with frequent and intense interpersonal contact with emotionally charged and nearly impossible to resolve client problems. Others (Cherniss 1980a, 1980b) would add as contributors of burnout "boredom, an excess of job demands, and organizational factors (e.g., role conflict, role ambiguity, and lack of participation in decision making)." The individual becomes "apathetic, cynical, and rigid [Cherniss 1980b:21]" (Whitehead & Lindquist 1986). Other researchers agree with Cherniss's opinion on the importance of administrative support for correctional officers (Jacobs and Kraft 1978; Lombardi 1981; Toch and Klofas 1982). According to Whitehead & Lindquist (1986), administrative sources of stress include "lack of clear guidelines for job performances, lack of communication from management, inoperable rules developed by persons unacquainted with the actual work setting."

Job burnout research pertaining to probation and parole found that burnout levels correlated with different seniority levels. Burnout in officers who were past their initial employment period increased as they reached about three years. However, officers with fifteen years or more experienced burnout levels as low as the newly hired officers (Whitehead 1985). A survey of twelve western states and Guam found that probation officers "reported being more stressed about those conditions (stressors) over which they had some locus of control" (paperwork perceived to be unnecessary, not enough time for job assignments, uncertainty about retirement benefits, family and financial worries, etc.) (Thomas 1988). Age appeared to have relevance, with the study finding that officers under thirty had the lowest burnout rates, whereas those in the 41-50 range had the highest. The burnout curve dropped in the 51-60 group. However, seniority or selection criteria rather than age proved to be the critical variable. This finding is said to contradict somewhat Maslach and Jackson's

(1981) finding that burnout is more likely early in one's career (Thomas 1988).

A number of factors unique to corrections contribute to burnout. For example, the correctional system has sometimes been criticized for being ineffective (Sechrest et al. 1979; Lipton et al. 1975); workers are unable to choose the clients (Ohlin et al. 1956). "At the level of the individual officer, awareness of burnout seems to be a logical first course of action" (Whitehead 1985). An effective orientation program is recommended to alleviate the reality shock for new officers (Kramer 1974) and allow them to begin work with a positive outlook. Further, it is helpful to assign experienced officers who are not burned out as mentors for newly hired officers (Whitehead 1985).

Burnout contributes to "the poor delivery of human services to people in need of them" (Thacker 1979). It also lowers employees' morale and increases absenteeism and job turnover. Additionally, "burnout correlates with other damaging indexes of human such as alcoholism, mental illness, marital conflict, and suicide. Such dysfunction seems to be especially prevalent in police and correctional workers . . ." (Thacker 1979). Maslach (1976) found that correctional officers rarely realized that the numerous physical problems (exhaustion, insomnia, ulcers, migraine headaches, neck and backaches, etc.) were psychosomatic. They used tranquilizers, drugs, or alcohol as coping devices.

A detention center staff psychologist, Jo Ann Thacker (1979), saw the solution to job stress as being "largely an educational one." Aggressive training programs should be implemented. What produces burnout, how it can affect professional and personal responsibilities, basic relaxation, and other techniques for reducing the stressfulness of working in corrections should be a part of the curriculum. Supportive counseling services are needed as follow-up to such training.

Research involving forty-one juvenile correctional workers found that the largest percentage of burnout resulted from staff anger. Weekly or biweekly staff meetings where employees could verbalize grievances and problems involving the juvenile clients was one suggested method of alleviating stress. Training sessions to define work roles and personal conflicts with the juvenile inmates were also recommended (Farmer 1988). According to research, older workers experience less stress than young workers. Gender did not appear significant, with men and women tending to be similar concerning burnout (Crosby 1982; Maslach 1982; Farmer 1988).

According to Manning (1983):

> Perhaps the best recent scholarly work on burnout in corrections was presented by Maslach (1976), Garte and Rosenblum (1978), and Thacker (1979). These scholars not only explain some of the causes but also offer ideas for dealing with this age-old problem. Maslach encourages burned-out correctional workers to actively express, analyze, and share their personal feelings with their colleagues. Thacker advocates an in-service training program. Garte and Rosenblum suggest the development of workshop exercises designed to blend work and leisure activities.

Correctional counselors' burnout problems are seen as resulting from perceived contrary objectives of "punishment and control" from society and "rehabilitation and helping them [inmates]" from the correctional institutions (Werner 1975). Kassebaum, Ward, and Wilner (1971) find difficulties as attributed to the "so-called dichotomy that has traditionally existed between custody and treatment forces in correctional institutions" (Manning 1983).

The peer support group has been seen as an effective strategy to minimize burnout. "Not only does this medium provide a forum for airing complaints, expressing feelings, and brainstorming solutions to problems, but the collective process supplies the staff member with a shared sense of professional identity" (Smith 1982). The in-service training environment involves peer interaction and is believed to satisfy the need for identity and support. Not only is the presence of peers effective, but the fact of the training site's separation from the work environment is believed to promote "support, empathy, and professional identity" (Smith 1982).

Overall, among the mechanisms advised for stress experienced by correctional professionals we find:

> Increased stress management training, professional counseling for officers and their families, peer advisement, and required fitness standards and programs have been identified as important measures that should be developed and implemented at the department level. The use of relaxation responses and neutralization techniques, proper nutrition and diet, and regular exercise, particularly aerobic exercise,

have been offered as remedies for the individual officer (Sewell 1984:520) (Sewell 1986).

It is important to ensure nutrition through a proper diet and a physical fitness program that includes exercise three to four nonconsecutive days each week, for twenty to thirty minutes at each session. Mental fitness (although the nutrition and physical factors just noted enhance both mental and physical fitness), and forms of meditation such as transcendental meditation, yen, yoga, and self-hypnosis are said to be effective. The following are "two major culminations of methods recommended by the National Institute of Mental Health and by Dr. John Stratton of the Los Angeles County Sheriff's Department" (Clements & Horn 1986):

National Institute of Mental Health

1. Work off stress by physical activity; do not allow stress to build up.
2. Talk and share worries and frustrations with someone you trust and respect; know when to ask for help before it becomes too late.
3. Learn to accept what you cannot change.
4. Avoid self-medication: the use of alcohol or drugs only masks stress; it does not relieve it.
5. Get enough sleep and rest; lack of sleep can lessen your ability to deal with stress.
6. Balance your time of work and relaxation. Schedule time for recreation so you can relax.
7. Do something for others. Too often we are caught up only with our problems; doing for others helps to act as a relief from this.
8. Take one thing at a time. Do not take on more work than you know you can handle.
9. Give in once in a while; do not always fight every battle as if your life depended on it.
10. Make yourself available; do not withdraw and become isolated. By getting involved, you do not have time to feel sorry for yourself and thus increase stress (U.S. Government 1972).

Dr. John Stratton

1. Eat breakfast.
2. No between-meal snacks. The body only needs and can only process so much food at one time. In addition, when you continually snack, especially with coffee and sweets, your body builds up excessive amounts of non-nutrients that help cause a variety of disorders.
3. Maintain your ideal body weight. When a person is frustrated or depressed, he may tend to lose weight. When extremely nervous, a person may tend to gain weight. When a person is overweight or underweight, body systems tend to degenerate or become overburdened. This may lead to wearing out or overloading of the body's ability to function.
4. No smoking. Smoking decreases the ability of the body to take in and process oxygen.
5. Moderate drinking. For every ounce of alcohol 10,000 brain cells die. Brain cells are not regenerated; once lost they do not return to a functional level. Other functions of the body are also affected.
6. Regular sleep. Be active every day; do not allow your body-mind system to sit idle all the time.

Leadership

The authors of *Megatrends 2000* have proclaimed the 1990s as a decade of *women in leadership*. They report that "the dominant principle of organizations has shifted from management in order to control an enterprise, to leadership in order to bring out the best in people and to respond quickly to change" (Naisbitt & Aburdene 1990). They talk about the differences between management and leadership that relate to orientation, mission, assumptions, behavior, organizational environments, and ultimately results. Among the leadership attributes required to meet the needs in the future are skills of a teacher, facilitator, and coach. There are many who feel that the new management attributes are seen as innately female.

Sally Helgesen, author of *The Female Advantage* (1990), has noted that one of the main gender differences is that women structure organizations as a web, or network, rather than a hierarchy. The woman executive, she found, places herself "in the center reaching out, rather than at the top reaching down."

As attitudes and views toward women change in society, so will they change for women in corrections. As more women reach the top, opportunities for women will increase at every level. During August 1990, the director of the Labor Department's Office of Federal Contract Compliance Programs (OFCCP) announced that her agency would enforce the laws and "shatter the glass ceiling." She noted that women and minorities get to certain levels, then don't appear to have equal opportunities. Her office would be about "enforcing equal opportunity laws for government contractors—a group that includes every company on the Fortune 500 list of the nation's largest corporations" (Swoboda 1990). Women in correctional employment constitute a valuable asset to the field of corrections.

Our journey is not and has not been easy. Like Alice, "it takes all the running we can do" to obtain and retain a measure of success. And if we want to advance in our careers, again like Alice, we "must run at least twice as fast as that." We have been diligent, persistent, enduring, and resilient. Now our horizon is widening. Therefore, it is time to reexamine our goals and revise them upward. Women in corrections are winners. According to James & Jongeward (1973), "Winners have different potentials. Achievement is not the most important thing. Authenticity is. The authentic person. . . is] a credible, responsive person." She appreciates the uniqueness of others even as she actualizes her own unprecedented uniqueness (James & Jongeward 1973). It is the responsibility of women in corrections to believe in Lombardi's luck and be prepared to meet the new opportunities. Along with competence, this preparation will include a positive attitude, self-esteem, and confidence.

The proper management of success generally involves retention of initial success, advancement, the balancing of personal and professional responsibilities, the management of stress, and the avoidance of professional burnout. We will thereby control our own destiny and be limited only by our lack of aspirations. Rest assured the correctional world is a lot richer for our being here, and with proper management of our success, the sky is the limit.

Notes

1. Recent court decisions continue the trend of increasing career opportunities for women employed in male institutions. For example, see *Timm v. Gunter*, 917 F. 2d 1093, 1101 n.10 (8th Cir. 1990). The U.S. 9th Circuit

Court of Appeals on January 23, 1991 set a new stand-
ard (reasonable woman) for sexual harassment cases,
Ellison v. Brady, No. 89-1548 (9th Cir. January 23, 1991)
(WESTLAW, 1991 WL4579).

2. In 1979, a study concerning women officers was undertaken in California and a nationwide study of
women officers in state male institutions was conducted by Joann B. Morton. Also a study of women in
correctional employment was conducted by the Center for Women's Policy Studies in Washington, D.C.

References

The American Woman 1990-91. 1990. Ford Foundation,
AT&T, Chevron USA, etc. as mentioned in Women's pay still
far behind men's group reports. *The Washington Post*. April 26,
1990 .

Bolles, R. 1990. *What color is your parachute? A practical
manual for job-hunters & career changers*. Berkeley, Cal.: Ten
Speed Press.

Braiker, H. B. 1988. Does superwoman have it worst? *Working Woman* (August): 65.

Cherniss, C. 1980a. *Professional burnout in human service organizations*. New York: Praeger.

Cherniss, C. 1980b. *Staff burnout: Job stress in the human services*. Beverly Hills, Cal.: Sage.

Clements, C. B., & W. G. Horn. 1986. Stress management in
law enforcement. *Police Studies* (Fall): 158.

Crosby, G. 1982. The stress burn-out relationship: A study
of university faculty. Unpublished doctoral dissertation.
Arizona State University, Tempe.

Farmer, J. A. 1988. Relationship between job burnout and
perceived inmate exploitation of juvenile correctional workers.
*International Journal of Offender Therapy and Comparative
Criminology* 32 (April): 71.

Feinman, C. 1980. *Women in the criminal justice system*. New
York: Praeger.

Flowers, R. B. 1987. Women and criminality, victim, offender, and practitioner. *Contributions in Criminology and Penol-
ogy*. Number 18. Westport, Connecticut: Greenwood Press.

Garte, Sumner H., & Mark L. Rosenblum. 1978. Lighting
fires in burned-out counselors. *The Personnel and Guidance Journal* 57(3).

Helgesen, Sally. 1990. *The female advantage*. New York: Doubleday.

Jacobs, J., & L. Kraft. 1978. Integrating the keepers: A comparison of black and white guards in Illinois. *Social Problems* 25: 304-318.

James, M., & D. Jongeward. 1973. Winners and losers. *Born to Win. Transactional analysis with Gestalt experiments*. Reading, Mass.: Addison-Wesley Publishing Company.

Kassebaum, Gene, D. A. Ward, & D. M. Wilner. 1971. *Prison treatment and parole survival*. New York: John Wiley.

Kent, D. 1990. Beyond thirtysomething. *Working Woman* (Sept.):150.

Korn, Lester. 1988. *The success profile*. New York: Simon and Schuster.

Kramer, M. 1974. *Reality shock: Why nurses leave nursing*. St. Louis: C. V. Mosby.

Lipton, D., R. Martinson, & J. Wilks. 1975. *The effectiveness of correctional treatment: A survey of treatment evaluation studies*. New York: Praeger.

Lombardi, L. 1981. *Guards imprisoned*. New York: Elsevier.

Manning, W. 1983. An underlying cause of burnout. *Corrections Today* (February):20.

Maslach, Christina. 1976. Burned out. *Human Behavior* (Sept): 16-22.

Maslach, C. 1982. *Burnout: The cost of caring*. Englewood Cliffs, N. J.: Prentice-Hall.

Maslach, C., & S. Jackson. 1981. The measurement of experienced burnout. *Journal of Occupational Behavior* 2:99-113.

McGarvey, R. 1988. The confidence factor. *Executive Female*. National Association for Female Executives 9 (4).

McLane, H. J. 1980. *Selecting, developing, and retaining women executives: A corporate strategy for the eighties*. New York: Litton Educational Publishing. As reviewed in the 1980 Monthly Labor Review (December): 71-72.

Naisbitt, J., and P. Aburdene. 1990. *Megatrends 2000*. New York: William Morrow and Company.

National Advisory Commission on Criminal Justice Standards and Goals, 1975. Standard 14.3, Employment of Women, reprinted in *Careers in the criminal justice system: Excerpts*, July:476-77.

National Woman Abuse Prevention Project. 1989. Answers to some commonly asked questions about domestic violence.

Understanding domestic violence: Fact Sheets. Washington, D.C.: National Woman Abuse Prevention Project.

Ohlin, L. E., H. Piven, & D. M. Pappenfort. 1956. Major dilemmas of the social worker in probation and parole. *National Probation and Parole Officer J. 2.* (July): 211-225.

Sechrest, L., S. O. White, & E. D. Brown (eds.). 1979. *The rehabilitation of criminal offenders: Problems and prospects.* Washington, D. C.: National Academy of Sciences.

Sewell, J. D. 1984. Stress in university enforcement. *The Journal of Higher Education* 55(4): 515-523.

Sewell, J. D. 1986. Administrative concerns in law enforcement stress management. *Police Studies* (Fall): 158.

Smith, J. O. 1982. Rekindling the flame. The use of inservice training as burnout prevention. *Federal Probation Quarterly* (June): 64.

Swoboda, F. August 28, 1990. Looking for a way to break the 'Glass Ceiling.' *The Washington Post.* Col. 3:A-15.

Thacker, J. 1979. Reducing burnout. *Corrections Today.* (November-December):50.

Thomas, R. L. 1988. Stress perception among select federal probation and pretrial services officers and their supervisors. *Federal Probation* (September):52.

Toch, H., & J. Klofas. 1982. Alienation and desire for job enrichment among correction officers. *Federal Probation* 46: 35-44.

Tunick, G. 1990. Continuing confessions. *Executive Female Magazine* (September/October):75.

Vobejda, B. 4 percent increase in U.S. childbirths seen. *Washington Post,* January 20, 1991.

Waitley, Denis. 1983. *The seeds of greatness.* Old Tappan, N. J.: Fleming H. Revell Co.

Werner, Ronald I. 1975. The criminal justice system at the breaking point. *Social Work* (November): 436-441.

Whitehead, J. T. 1985. Job burnout in probation and parole. Its extent and intervention implications. *Criminal Justice Behavior* 12 (March):91-110.

Whitehead, J. T., and C. A. Lindquist. 1986. Correctional officer job burnout: a path model. *Journal of Research in Crime and Delinquency* 23 (February): 25-26.

Black Women in Correctional Employment

Jess Maghan, Ph.D., and
Leasa McLeish-Blackwell, M. P. A

The record and extent of female employment is now of sufficient duration and diversity to merit specific inquiry on black women who work in corrections.* A portrayal of their experience can be useful. It can provide a support system for women and an educational resource for all employees. Although this paper focuses primarily on the black woman as uniformed correctional officer and supervisor, there is another whole story to be told of women who are not uniformed employees. Black women in direct inmate contact positions—counselors, paralegals, attorneys, law librarians, food service workers, clerical and support staff, medical and mental health personnel, educators, chaplains, volunteers, inmate grievance officers, ombudspersons, hearing officers—have a major impact on the quality of institutional life. In many cases, these categories of employees functioned in positions of direct inmate contact long before women gained full status under Title VII as uniformed correctional officers.

Despite irrational fears held by some concerning the reasons that attract women to correctional employment, it has become apparent that occupational choice factors for women are the same as those for men (Lundman 1984; Zimmer 1986; Maghan 1988; Gilbert 1990). Although these reasons may be the same, the adjustment and survival issues for women have been distinct and difficult, particularly for black women, who are equally inspiring in their determination to succeed.

Pike (1985) highlights the dynamic of being both black and a woman in the law enforcement environment. Both groups are seen to have been recruited to serve "people like themselves." Pike, therefore, views race, like gender, as a visible characteristic and prejudice as a dimension of organizational life.

We have adhered to the term black female to meet the editorial theme of this chapter. However, the current terminology in use by and with Americans of African descent is African-American.

However, she points out that black men do not challenge the "quintessential officer role in the same way women do."

> One can be black, yet be strong, streetwise, and masculine. The symmetry or dependency of what women are like in contrast to macho officers means that it is far less likely that women successfully meet the ideal type . . . Blacks [males] and women are also different with respect to organizational adaptation.

> Since separate but equal was declared unconstitutional, no organizational (facility, uniform, or program) changes are necessary to incorporate blacks [males]. Sex norms (co-ed locker rooms?) present a very different type of barrier, which at least directs organizations to different strategies of adaptation.

Pike further observes (with respect to black roles) that prejudice against blacks has different consequences than prejudice against women. She, like Zimmer (1986) and Maghan (1988), feels that the further understanding of female recruit officers and their retention will provide guidance on the total impact of both race and sex.

Sociologists and others have written extensively of the matriarchal role of the black woman within the African-American cultural and familial milieu (Bianchi and Spain 1986). The transference of this dynamic within the essential interactive officer-inmate and inmate-inmate context of correctional work—especially in a highly distilled environment of predominantly young, minority male inmates—merits further research. Black female entry-level employees generally carry higher levels of educational achievement, but the relationship of this factor to their choice and attitudes toward correctional work remain untapped.

Pervasive invidious distinctions based on gender, which have prescribed specific kinds of employment roles for women, may legitimately affect black women's perceptions of their roles in the correctional work force. These women may come to the correctional officer role anticipating that the expectations of the department may be circumscribed by race or gender and defined accordingly. Hence, their perceptions of their roles within the corrections department are likely to reflect some of the sexual discrimination they have internalized and expect.

Facilities and Policy Improvements

The integration of female correctional officers into the national correctional work force has had a positive humanizing effect. The presence of women in the work force has initiated changes in every aspect of correctional operations: physical plant, personnel, and programs. Correctional architecture now must accommodate a mixed-gender work force. New mixed-gender physical plant features include showers and toilet facilities constructed with waist-level security bands, open dorms, and, in New York City, a newly constructed nursery for infants under the age of one.

The New York City Department of Correction has recently opened the Rose M. Singer Correctional Center, a unisex jail where male officers guard female inmates. The same concerns regarding privacy rights of female inmates surfaced in the deployment of male officers in this facility. This situation was resolved by determining that the privacy rights of female inmates could be protected, without discriminating against male correctional officers, by permitting female inmates to cover cell windows for fifteen minute intervals and by issuing suitable nighttime garments (621 Fed. 1210 U.S. Court of Appeals, May 8, 1990). These programmatic and architectural adjustments clearly illustrate the positive effect of a mixed-gender work force on the policy and operational standards of the department. These adjustments were made readily adaptable out of the long-time experience of having female correctional officers assigned to male jails.

The capacity of correctional agencies to accommodate these changes is commendable and clearly shows the integration of legal and social issues affecting both employees and inmates. The impact of these changes is further substantiated in the gender-free language of operational procedures, training course content, public information bulletins, and inmate rule books. As in the case of the nation's police departments— where the occupational titles of "patrolman" and "policeman" are changing to "police officer"—within correctional agencies there is to be *no* gender distinction. This situation is further secured through interpersonal communication skills for staff in their interaction with each other and inmates. Finally, the more precise body of recent sexual harassment and human rights law has further secured these interactions on a civil and equal basis: no distinction in terms of gender is tolerated.

When one views these changes from a positive perspective, the enormous and continuous changes in the structural, social, and interactive aspects of the entry and influence of the black woman in correctional employment offers possibilities for enhancing and achieving a more effective and humane correctional environment.

A vivid illustration of these changes from a new generation employee is found in the valedictorian speech of Phyllis Spence, a black probationary correctional officer, at her Correction Academy graduation ceremony in May 1990. This speech was published in *New York Newsday*, a daily newspaper with readership in the five boroughs of the City.

> Before joining the department, I believed that the different law enforcement agencies were viewed as separate but equal. I now see that the Department of Correction is considered a lower class of law enforcement than the others. And it is upsetting but not surprising that the group receiving the least respect is the one comprised largely of African-Americans and Hispanics.
>
> Thus, correction officers have a special obligation not to forget that society is still full of racism, and that it affects them as well as the inmates under their control. As C.O.s we can afford to send our children to better schools if we so choose, but we must not forget our brothers and sisters who cannot, and we must fight for their children also, if we do so only out of the fear that a deprived child may harm our own.
>
> Our country must overcome its racism and take responsibility for all its children. We must see to it that every single child, regardless of race, color, creed, or socioeconomic status, receives an equal opportunity not just to survive, but to thrive. Then and only then will the demand for "institutions of confinement" decline, and the quality of our lives take a turn for the better.

The Past is Prologue

There are marked parallels in the emergent mixed-gender work force of police and correctional services. Both have rich occupational histories of early female pioneers in their respective fields. Several remarkable female wardens and commissioners actually supervised and administered the exclusively male prison systems in the late 19th and early 20th centuries (Feinman 1980; Breed 1980). However, the presence of women as line workers and first-line supervisors in adult male correctional facilities was virtually nonexistent. Prior to the promulgation of Title VII of the Civil Rights Act in the 1970s, most female line employees in police and correctional agencies were restricted to the women's bureau and exclusively handled juvenile and female adult inmates. Further, the employment of these women was usually racially segregated (Moeller and Travisono 1983).

These early examples of female employment, though narrowly contrived and controlled, laid the groundwork for establishing the bona fide occupational qualification of women to serve as correctional officers and supervisors. However, the application of the impact of these historic female roles in relation to the modern-day work force is limited. It is not until the mandated and deliberate Title VII staging of a minority and mixed-gender work force in the late 1960s and 1970s, with women entering as full-fledged correctional officers, that distinct organizational and cultural changes can be discerned. It is here that black women in correctional employment were recognized as a modern-day pioneer group in the increasingly diverse American correctional work force.

When women began entering the correctional work force through Title VII protections, the primary concern was how to guarantee staff safety and inmates' privacy while ensuring women officers' right to full employment. From the beginning, correctional administrators were primarily concerned about women's ability to guard male inmates. Ironically, this was not a concern of the inmates. Lynn Zimmer (1986) conducted an extensive survey of female correctional officers in the New York State Department of Correctional Services. Her work is an in-depth study of the emergent mixed-gender work force in a state prison system. Zimmer writes:

> The members of the prison community who reacted most favorably to the hiring of female guards were the inmates whom women were required to control. Although they had to accommodate women's presence by making some adjustments in their own behavior—most notably, taking precautions to protect their own privacy—most inmates did not consider these adjustments difficult or unreasonable.

These concerns, initially perceived as intractable, were eventually declared by the courts as the responsibility of corrections officials to resolve by devising operational plans to protect inmate privacy while maximizing equal opportunities for women (*Bowling v. Enomoto; Forts v. Ward*). Subsequent statistical evidence verifies that fears concerning safety of female officers were unfounded. The number of women assaulted in the line of duty has not been disproportionate to the number of men. Most of the assaults or line-of-duty deaths have occurred out of general inmate violence situations and were not gender-based.

The birth of a mutual awareness and interest in the conditions of confinement, and thus the conditions of work, creates a groundwork for building a mixed-gender work force that better serves both the keeper and the kept. Maghan (1981) states:

> Prisoners' rights and the officers' working environment are inseparably linked. Improvement in one affects the other. In getting both to see their community of interest lies the promise of adding meaning to attempts to reduce the tension, confusion, and danger they mutually face.

From this bridge of mutuality of interests, correctional officers of both genders, all races and ethnic groups, veterans and neophytes, can collaborate to achieve the common mission: safe and secure correctional facilities. Gradually, correctional agencies have discovered that the mutuality of occupational choice factors can provide a platform of commonality of interests. These interests can be deployed into strategies and training sessions to bridge perceived differences between male and female officers. Creative ventures for managing the mixed-gender work environment can serve to heighten the opportunities for all officers.

Jacqueline Pitts, a black assistant deputy warden, designed the NYC Department of Correction's mandatory in-service course for all incumbent correction officers, "Reduce Violence, Promote Safety" (RVPS). One segment of this course specifically addresses the role of black women (and other ethnicities), using interactive dialogue with all the class participants. In this segment of the course, black female officers are asked to voice their feelings of role obfuscation as well as front-line performance and successes. The pros and cons of these situations are then listed and discussed by the class. At the end of the discussion, all participants have a better understanding of their common struggles and desires for enhanced working associations. For example, to promote better quality of worklife, women have stated that they are equal to men, yet they are infrequently selected to don protective equipment in order to use physical force during inmate disturbances. Supervisors and officers, both male and female, discuss this issue, and at the conclusion of the class all participants are more aware of such inconsistencies. The desire of black women to be recognized on par with other officers leads to an awareness to ensure that women officers of all ethnicities are utilized in emergency preparedness training and intervention at the line and first-line supervisory level.

This similarity of concern over occupational identity and vision affirms a basic principle of human relations: everyone, regardless of race or gender, wants what everyone else wants—to be heard and to make a difference. If the most important factors in the decision of black women to become correctional officers are the same as those of women and men of all races, then the foundation for further alliances is evident.

New York Profile

The New York City Department of Correction serves as a pilot bellwether for this discussion. The department has a rich and long tradition of employing black women. Statistics from the NYC Department of Correction well substantiate a marked and continued growth of women, especially black women, into the work force. For example, in 1984 LaSalle reported that of the 6,039 correctional officers in New York City, only 921 (18 percent) were women. (LaSalle did not provide statistics on black female representation in the uniformed ranks.) In September 1990, the official department census placed the total correctional officer work force at 11,537. Of this number, 3,394 were women, and 2,851 (24.7 percent) were black women. (Additionally, black women comprise 31 percent of the civilian work force in the department.)

As of January 1991, the department has one black woman warden, three deputy wardens, and nine assistant deputy wardens, as well as one hundred captains as first-line supervisors. The September 1990 equal employment report for the agency documented a continued marked increase in the employment of all women: 2,851 black officers, 349 Hispanic officers, 189 white officers, and six Asian officers, for a combined total of 3,394 female officers, or 29.4 percent of the department's uniformed work force.

A Profile of Black Women in Correctional Employment

The McLeish-Blackwell (1990) profile of the black female correctional officer reaffirms the mutuality of these occupational choice factors. (See Table 1.) This survey was also administered to supervisory and civilian personnel, male and female, with similar results.

The McLeish-Blackwell profile is consistent with the general profile of women entering law enforcement. Table 2 profiles the most important factors in the decision to become a police officer.

Similar occupational choice factors between women and men are emerging in other traditionally male-dominated trades and craft skill occupations. For example, there is an extensive movement of black women entering the construction and transportation industries in both New York City and nationally. As Table 1 indicates, women choose correctional employment for financial security. Career advancement is realized more in the Correction Department than in the New York City Police Department. This phenomenon can be attributed to the size of both agencies, but perhaps more directly to the variety of posts available in the correctional environment. This pattern of more rapid career advancement in the corrections field appears to hold in other regions of the country as well.

The significance of the McLeish-Blackwell profile is confirmed by the socioeconomic status of black women in American society. The percentage of black women who are the head of their households has historically been much higher than for any other racial/ethnic group surveyed (Clark 1963; Lerner 1973). In 1984, 44 percent of all black American families were headed by women, compared to only 23.2 percent of Hispanic families, and 13 percent of white families. Furthermore, the income for minorities is lower than the income for white women or men (LaSalle 1984). These factors reiterate that the black woman, as head of her family, will direct her energies to those areas where there is a solid equal employment ground, good benefits, and the opportunity to earn a pay comparable to that of her male counterparts.

One black woman with over fifteen years in the department comments: "I had to support my two children. We worked hard. All I was concerned about at that time (1975) was making enough to support my children and myself."

Table 1
Most Important Factor In Decision To Become a
Correctional Officer (Black Female)

N = 43 Responses	No. of Responses	Percentage
Salary	17	39.5
Benefits	7	16
Selected from other Civil Service listing	5	11.6
Needed a job	4	9
Better opportunity	3	7
Liked CJS/Law enforcement	3	7
Helping others	2	4.7
Advancement	1	2
Family tradition/ Civil Service	1	2
Challenging	1	2
Security	1	2
Change from typical office job	1	2
Other	1	2

Table 2
Most Important Factors In Decision To Become a Police Officer By Female and Male NYPD Recruit Officers

	Female	Male	P-Level
Ability to help people	2.92 (1)	2.90 (1)	n.s.
Ability to work directly with people	2.86 (2)	2.76 (2)	.001
Challenge of police work	2.76 (3)	2.76 (3)	n.s.
Chance to experience working in the community	2.74 (4)	2.62 (4)	.001
Pay as a police officer	2.47 (5)	2.47 (6)	n.s.
Excitement of police work	2.43 (6)	2.54 (5)	.01
It just seemed like a good job opportunity	2.42 (7)	2.32 (9)	.02
Have always wanted to be a police officer	2.28 (8)	2.45 (7)	.001
Chance to work outdoors	2.21 (9)	2.35 (8)	.01
Freedom of the job	1.91 (10)	1.89 (10)	n.s.
Recruitment info from police department	1.85 (11)	1.78 (11)	n.s.
Influence of friends or relatives who are police officers	1.72 (12)	1.73 (12)	n.s.
Influence of friends or relatives who are not police officers	1.57 (13)	1.55 (14)	n.s.
Wearing a uniform	1.55 (14)	1.70 (13)	.001
Carrying a gun	1.47 (15)	1.42 (15)	n.s.
We've always had a police officer in the family	1.26 (16)	1.29 (16)	n.s.

Today, as was the case in 1975, the Department of Correction provides the potential for realizing desired familial economic benefits. The entry salary for a correctional officer in New York City is approximately $26,000, in addition to the full benefits of a twenty-year retirement package, unlimited sick leave, uniform allowance, and excellent access to upward mobility for those who prepare themselves for promotional exams. For the black woman who meets the age and educational requirement of G.E.D. or high school graduate, this salary, benefits, and occupational career path represent an exceptional opportunity for economic security. Many of the black women surveyed reported leaving other employment to accept the position of correctional officer because of these benefits.

Nonetheless, unique circumstances still exist. Often in a single parent family situation, the black woman is confronted with organizing her personal life and family responsibilities around the requirements of shift work, rotating wheel assignments, and traveling to the various facilities of the department. These may not be unique problems, but they illustrate that the adjustment to the work culture and organization of correctional employment is particularly acute for the black woman in her family role. This situation is vividly portrayed in this study: Forty-six percent of the women surveyed were not married, and 43 percent were the main wage earner in their households.

Again, a poignant profile of their adjustment to the work schedule of correctional service is offered by the following comments of the officers surveyed in November 1990 in response to the question, "Were there unique circumstances with which the African-American female had to cope?":

- Starting this job at the age of twenty-one, the entire department is an experience.
- I am a single mother. The time spent away from my son was difficult, although I am fortunate enough to have a supportive family.
- Having to be separated from my child and family for long hours, and "wheeling" are terrible for raising a child.
- One has to experience this job: for me, taking orders from people that have a cold behavior was tough.
- The stressful situations, sensory deprivation, mandatory overtime, excessive dealing with a

criminal subculture, [and] . . . the paramilitary setting are unique.

- Having to notify [an] inmate/officer of the death of a loved one . . . [is] very difficult.
- Seeing an inmate denied the right to go to his mother's or a close relative's funeral home "viewing" was difficult to deal with.
- At times, I felt that I was in danger from inmates that I supervised. I never felt that way before, I never felt danger before.
- Spouse difficulties became job related: seeing me in uniform [was] a threat at first [and] hard to understand.

Others cited "having to fight to protect coworkers"; being alienated "by a group for not agreeing with negative behaviors"; and "realizing that I am locked in with criminals" as unique situations they've encountered.

Many of the black women surveyed shared experiences of frustrated spouses or partners who did not understand why a woman would choose to be a correctional officer. The vestiges of wearing a uniform, carrying a gun, being an authority figure, and having economic dependence on the female partner are but a few of the common frustrations expressed by the male partners of black female correctional officers. However, this situation is not restricted to the male side of the relationship. Many of the black female officers surveyed shared a new sense of isolation and suffering related to assuming the role of a uniformed correctional officer. This isolation was expressed as a void that even friends on the job cannot fill. While this sense of occupational isolation is a common phenomenon of the correctional officer (especially the neophyte officer), it is also particularly difficult for the female officer and is often compounded for the black female officer as a minority within a minority.

Another situation shared by the black women officers of this study was a concern for the increasing incarceration rate of young African-American males. Many of the women cited situations where family members or members of the families of intimate friends or neighbors were incarcerated. There was a unanimous concern for the concomitant stress and emotional pain experienced by this situation in their lives on and off the job.

"African-American," vis-a-vis the term "black," is considered more appropriate and sensitive to the contemporary identity and vision of Americans of African descent. In this context, other scenarios of job identity and stress can occur.

As African-American women learn more about their heritage and become more self-confident, some choose to wear the traditional African dress and groom their hair in a manner that is not consistent with Western culture. Uniforms are the standard wear for security personnel in New York City and many other correctional facilities; therefore, that is consistent. Some African-American women, however, choose to wear their hair in "locks," a hairstyle indigenous to descendants of Africa. The hairstyle alone may cause the wearer to experience a certain aloofness at first and some discriminatory behavior from both acquaintances and persons in authority. In many instances, the aloofness and discriminatory acts emanate from other African-Americans. Individuals from other cultures are often more accepting of the African-American officer's expression of her identity. With more and more women opting to wear locks, coworkers and persons in authority must begin to accept these women for their abilities and capabilities and not deny them posts or positions based on a narrowly contrived, misinformed perception. This and similar situations will, of course, adjust over time as the mixed-gender, multicultural work force becomes more entrenched in the correctional environment.

The Black Woman as a Correctional Supervisor

The basic role of a supervisor in a criminal justice agency is to assume the responsibility of directing a work group's activities, to heighten the job satisfaction of subordinates, and optimize the effectiveness of the group (Weston 1979). Entering the supervisory ranks requires successful line performance in terms of attendance and disciplinary record and often the passing of a civil service exam. This selection process may affect women in the following manner:

1. Women, who are usually the last to be hired, have less time on the job and therefore may not be eligible through their seniority to be selected as provisional captains.
2. Those women who were not working in male facilities may have been limited in their knowledge of certain rules when working in a male facility.

3. In an effort to be a successful captain's candidate, the officer must make a concerted effort to acquire up-dated rules and regulations so that she may study them. There is a large proportion of single mothers or single heads of households. The stress of family responsibilities interferes with concerted study, resulting in low scores and thus placing the candidate at the bottom of the promotion list.

4. She may now have a steady post that she likes, earning needed overtime hours. Upon promotion she will have to start from the bottom again: "going on the wheel." This may disrupt personal and family life.

5. A woman in an abusive domestic situation may be so intimidated by her spouse that she does not take the promotion exam or accept promotion achieved. The spouse resents her earning a higher salary or carrying a higher prestige. This is a threat to his masculinity.

The question, "Are there any similarities or differences when one is supervised by persons of the opposite sex?" was asked of the black women supervisors surveyed. The majority answered that there was *no* difference. An informal poll of men and women within the department revealed that correctional officers respect supervisors who are able to make sound decisions, act fairly, show respect, and give sound direction to their subordinates. The supervisor should also support subordinates when necessary and generally set a good example for the assigned housing area. These people indicated that if the superior acted in such a manner, then that person—whether a man or a woman—would have their respect.

Of those who cited differences, the observations were that men tend to be "uneasy" working with women supervisors and often did not like a woman "telling them what to do." However, there were only a few who believed men perceived women as a threat, especially white men. One black woman with over five years as a first-line supervisor stated, "There is a preconceived idea from males as to how I *should* approach various situations or how I *will* respond; and, therefore, they are surprised by my take-charge attitude and performance. "

In general, the black women surveyed for this study stated, "As long as you work hard, are responsible, gain respect of your peers and supervisors (irrespective of gender or race), you will succeed." It is significant that among the assistant deputy wardens (the senior administrative rank surveyed for this study) the consensus held that there were *no* differences in being supervised by women of different cultures or races. This response came from a group of men, of which 46 percent were white, 36 percent black, and 18 percent Hispanic. Nonetheless, a perception that each group was receiving better treatment than the other persisted. This perception clearly shows that the separation of values and identities is still a very real phenomenon in the work culture. It will require extensive training and work exposure to build more collegial and collaborative role fulfillment by both genders of all racial groups in the department.

The Black Female Officer and the Minority Inmate Population

Overshadowing the influx of black women in correctional employment is the proportion of the national inmate population that is increasingly nonwhite. The minority incarceration rate is higher than it has ever been since the invention of the penitentiary system (Christianson 1981). The United States Department of Justice's Bureau of Justice Statistics reports that black men constituted 43 percent of the national jail inmate population in 1989, up from 38 percent in 1987. The presence and interaction of black women correctional officers with this increasingly minority inmate population represents important role model and human relations staff development resources. Therefore, the black female correctional officer stands at a significant position in the examination of the racial composition of the nation's inmate population. Scant research has been undertaken concerning aspects of their occupational choice, socialization into the correctional officer work culture, as well as eventual full integration into the correctional work force.

When the inmate population is comprised predominantly of African-American and other minority groups, the challenge confronting the black woman becomes heightened. Cultural and family role modeling may come into play in a way that could impede or enhance her role. Black women are equal employees who, when working in direct service situations, provide unique benefits that may be capitalized on through training forums and increased awareness. Jewelle Taylor Gibbs (1988) reports:

> Young black males in contemporary American society have been miseducated by the educational system, mishandled by the criminal justice system, mislabeled by the mental health system, and mistreated by the social welfare system. All the major institutions of this

society have failed to respond appropriately and effectively to their multiple needs and problems.

Generally, female officers are less encumbered by the social restraints concerning expression of emotions imposed by sex role expectations; they may feel more comfortable with the expression and reception of feelings than some male staff. These and other attributes suggest the rich potential of further inquiry on the subject of the mixed-gender correctional work force.

Black Women and Upper Echelon Command

The record of black female incumbents in upper echelon management of the New York City Correction Department has always been exceptional. The first woman commissioner in New York City was Katherine Davis (1914-1915). Others were Burdette Lewis (1915-1917); Anna M. Kross (1954-1966); and Jacqueline Montgomery McMickens (1984-1986), the first black woman appointed commissioner. Commissioner McMickens appointed another black officer, Gloria Lee, as Chief of Department, the highest ranking uniformed post in the agency. McMickens and Lee are unique in that they rose through the ranks from correctional officers to the highest command positions of the agency.

The record of appointments to black women throughout the country in correctional employment during the past two decades has been noteworthy. Most agencies now have black women employed as upper echelon administrators, commissioners, directors, and legal counsel. The stories of modern day pioneers—such as Ruth Rushen, Helen Corrothers, and Jacqueline McMickens—can now be paralleled throughout the nation. Each had to experience the lonely spot at the top . . . a spot made more lonely by being the first black woman at the helm of major correctional agencies. Although they each experienced difficulties because of their unique standing, they survived and established powerful role models for the increasing contingency of black women in the correctional work force.

Commissioner Jacqueline McMickens, in a speech to the NYC Women In Correction organization in March 1990, proffered this advice:

> Learn to negotiate. Correctional service is an incredible field for women. Women are having a difficult time (as others are) in learning the craft of career

ladder achievement. Nevertheless, networking is not only an upward spiral; in addition to those who are above you in rank, look always among your peers for mentors, because no one person knows everything. Learn all you can; go back to school and continue your education. The only competition is . . . yourself.

Black women must fully recognize their pivotal role in determining the quality of life for both the officer and the inmate. Their increasing number in the national correctional work force is significant. As Commissioner McMickens counseled, these women must learn to negotiate—with each other and with their male counterparts. Black women employees bring an array of new and unique cultural and human relations insights to the role of correctional officer. Agencies need to develop innovative ways to tap these talents in the interests of enhancing the custodial care of inmates and to more fully develop the job fulfillment of not only the black female officer but of all correctional employees.

References

American Correctional Association. 1983. *The American prison from the beginning: A pictorial history.* College Park, Md.: American Correctional Association.

Bianchi, Susanne, and Daphne Spain. 1986. *American women in transition.* New York: Russell Sage Foundation.

Bowling v. Enonoto. 514 F. Supp. 201 (1981).

Breed, Allen F. 1980. *Women in correctional employment.* Washington, D.C.: National Institute of Corrections.

Christianson, Scott. 1981. Our black prisons. *Crime and Delinquency,* Vol 27: 364-75.

Clark, Kenneth B. 1965. Sex and status. In Robert Staples (ed), *The black family: Essays and studies.* Belmont, Cal.: Wadsworth Publishing Company, Inc.

Feinman, Clarice. 1980. *Women in criminal justice.* CBS Educational and Professional Publishing.

Fonts v. Ward. 621 F. 2d 1210 (1980).

Gibbs, Jewelle T. 1988. *Young, black, and male in America. An endangered Species,* Dover, Mass.: Auburn House Publishing Co.

Gilbert, Michael. 1990. *Working the unit: An inquiry into the discretionary behavior of correction officers.* Tempe, Ariz.: Arizona State University.

Lasalle, Robert. 1987. *Statistics on women, minorities in public administration.* Albany, N.Y.: New York State Division for Women.

Lerner, Gerder. 1973. *Black women in white America, A documentary history.*

Lundman, Richard J. 1984. *Police and policing.* New York: Holt, Rinehart and Winston.

McLeish-Blackwell, Leasa. 1990. *Upward mobility of female supervisors within the New York City Department of Correction.* Greenvale, N.Y.: C.W. Post University.

McMickens, Jacqueline Montgomery. September 1990. Address to the NYC Women In Correction Association (Unpublished). New York.

Maghan, Jess. 1988. *The 21st century cop: Police recruit perceptions as a function of occupational socialization.* Ann Arbor, Mich.: UMI Press.

Maghan, Jess. 1981. Guarding in prison. In David Fogel and Joe Hudson (eds). *Justice as fairness, perspectives on the justice model.* Cincinnati, Oh.: Anderson Publishing Company.

Pike, Diane Lovewell. 1985. Women in police academy training: Some aspects of organizational response. In Imogene L. Moyer (ed.), *The changing roles of women in the criminal justice system, offenders, victims, and professionals.* Prospect Heights, Ill.: Waveland Press.

Pitts, Jacqueline. 1990. *Reduce violence promote safety* (Curriculum). New York: New York City Department of Correction, Training Academy.

New York City Department of Correction. September 1990. *Work force summary analysis (uniformed).* New York: New York City Department of Correction.

Spence, Phyllis. 1990. Rikers, racism and disrespect. *Newsday* (October 12): 74.

The Correctional Association of New York. 1990. Women in prison: Fact sheet. New York: The Correctional Association of New York.

Weston, Paul B. 1978. *Supervision in the administration of justice.* Springfield, Ill.: Charles C Thomas.

Zimmer, Lynn. 1986. *Women guarding men.* Chicago: University of Chicago Press.

Women's Changing Roles in Corrections

Mary G. Hawkes, Ph.D.

Women's roles in correctional employment have changed dramatically from the onset of the women's reformatory movement at the end of the nineteenth century. The roles women have played in corrections, from 1870 to the present, have been influenced by major societal changes that fall into three time periods—1870 to 1935, 1935 to 1970, and 1970 to 1990. Traditionally, women's roles in the correctional field have been concerned with the treatment of juveniles and adult female offenders; therefore, the interplay of the roles of women staff and treatment of female offenders will be looked at during these periods.

Principle XXXVII of the Declaration of Principles Adapted and Promulgated by the National Congress on Penitentiary and Reformatory Discipline, 1870, states:

> This Congress is of the opinion that, both in the official administration of such a (prison) system, and in the voluntary co-operation of therein, the agency of women may be employed to excellent effect (Wines 1971, 547).

Women were, of course, employed as matrons in juvenile reform schools and women's quarters in prisons prior to 1870. One administrator who stands out was Eliza Farnum, who served as chief matron of the Mount Pleasant Female Prison at Ossining, New York, from 1844 to 1847. It was, however, the women's reformatory movement at the end of the nineteenth century that called for the removal of women from institutions designed to hold men and the establishment of separate prisons for women, *administered and staffed by women*.

Women's Reformatory Movement—1870 to 1935

The women's reformatory movement was shaped by several factors, including the following:

- social feminism aimed at improving the lot of 'the dependent and defective classes' and other disenfranchised groups
- social purity—a national campaign to clean out saloons, stamp out vice, raise standards of sexual morality, and strengthen the American home
- the treatment of juvenile delinquents in reform schools under the doctrine of 'parens patriae', which justified state intervention in family situations that seemed to encourage delinquency
- a new image of the female offender from the criminal beyond redemption . . . to the childlike, wayward, and redeemable fallen woman who was more sinned against than a sinner herself (Rafter 1990)

The major force behind the rallying call for separate reformatories for women were women's groups such as the General Federation of Women's Clubs, the Women's Christian Temperance Union, and church organizations. In each state, prominent women citizens, often of considerable means and influence, lobbied legislators and governors to enact legislation to establish a women's reformatory and provide the necessary funding.

At the first Congress of the National Prison Association in 1870, the following resolution was passed:

Resolved, that this Congress is of the opinion that separate prisons should be established for women, and that neither in city, county, nor state prisons should women be incarcerated with men; and further, that women should have charge of the female department in all cases where the sexes are imprisoned within the same enclosure (Wines 1871, 569).

In 1873 the Indiana Women's Prison was opened, and in 1877 the Massachusetts Prison for Women opened. These were separate from men's institutions in administration and location. Their architecture and operation in the beginning resembled the male custodial prison. They did, however, set the stage for the establishment of other separate institutions for women. Seventeen women's reformatories were opened between 1900 and 1933 in the midwest, northeast, south, and California.

The early women reformers called for the reformatories to be managed by specially trained, intelligent women who would serve as constructive role models for their charges. The first women superintendents had college degrees, and several held advanced degrees including law, medicine, and the Ph.D. Indeed, their education was superior to that of most of their male counterparts.

The position of matron was established in the early nineteenth century "because female prisoners by nature needed special treatment that only other women could provide and (to serve as) role models and thus effect positive change in their charges" (Rafter 1990, 14). The title "matron" survived until the middle of the twentieth century, when it was changed to "cottage officer" or "cottage warden" to reflect more professionalism. The only men employed on a full-time basis in women's reformatories were hired for heavy maintenance work.

The embodiment of the reformatory ideal was the cottage plan, modeled after juvenile reform schools, where the women could be reformed through domestic training. A rural location was considered desirable since "rural life was moral life" (Rafter 1990, 35). The superintendents and matrons lived on the grounds, usually in the same buildings with the inmates. A homelike atmosphere with the staff as "good" parental models pervaded the ideals.

Creative Leadership, Lack of Funds, Lack of Concern

Legislatures that enacted laws establishing women's reformatories failed to appropriate adequate funds for maintaining and operating them. The institutions were small, and the female inmates posed little threat to society. The state controlling authorities paid little attention to them. The lack of funds and lack of concern on the part of the central office created a situation that some of the more daring and imaginative superintendents used to develop programs far in advance of the time.

For example, without adequate staff at the New Jersey Reformatory, the first superintendent had to rely on more mature and stable inmates to supervise laundry and sewing departments. Thus, the seeds of inmate self-government and an honor system were sown. Some of the necessary light construction work was performed by the inmates and turned into arithmetic lessons. Katherine Bement Davis, the first superintendent at Bedford Hills, New York, allocated resources so that inmates could be trained for nontraditional jobs. Before the end of the nineteenth century, women at Framingham in Massachusetts earned indenture status (work release) to work in the community in domestic settings and later in commercial ones.

Not all the women superintendents experimented with innovative programs; even where this had occurred many were forced to curtail these activities when their inmate populations grew far beyond their physical capacities, necessary funds were not appropriated, and central controlling authorities became more suspicious of the avant garde methods used at women's institutions.

Perhaps the most important factor in the demise of the reformatory ideals was the necessity to admit women committed for serious felonies. Until the late twenties or early thirties, most states with women's reformatories also operated a small unit for the "more serious women criminals" at their state prison. Male wardens considered the women a nuisance, and as their prisons became crowded, they pressured to have the women transferred to the state reformatories. Thus, by 1935, "the women's reformatory ceased to exist in all but name"(Rafter 1990, 81). There were no protests from reform-minded women's groups. The country was deep into the Depression, and social reform movements with progressive ideals were put aside. In a few cases, the enlightened and adventuresome women superintendents continued their progressive methods and were eager to accept all the women formerly sent to the male prison.

From Matrons to Cottage Officers to Corrections Officers: 1935 - 1970

As noted earlier, the early superintendents and staff were usually required to live on the grounds of their institutions. The New Jersey Act of 1910 to Establish a State Reformatory for Women specifies, "The superintendent shall reside at all times within the precincts or dependencies of the reformatory . . ." Other full-time staff also lived there. They were on duty twenty-four hours a day.

When the New Jersey Reformatory for Women opened in January 1913, there were, as well as the superintendent, a nurse, housekeeper, and utility man. By the end of the year, a woman farmer had been added. Although these staff were trained to handle their particular departments, they had to be flexible and willing to help out in all the work.

Where Civil Service laws were in existence, staff appointments other than the superintendent were made in accordance with these laws. Superintendents were hired and served at the pleasure of the commissioner or director of corrections or the boards of commissioners of individual institutions.

In New Jersey in the 1930s, the title of "matron" was replaced by "occupational supervisor" for those women whose responsibilities were in the cottages. In California they were called "cottage wardens." Other titles were specific to the occupation—nurse, teacher, sewing supervisor, etc. By the 1940s, occupational supervisors in New Jersey became cottage officers or cottage supervisors. These titles remained until the 1970s, when they became, with their male counterparts in the institutions, correctional officers.

Before the 1970s, the titles and the roles played by the women staff were different from those of the male prison guard or correctional officer. Major qualifications for male prison guards during this period were "brute strength and ability to shoot," while for female cottage officers their "strength must be of the spirit" (Close 1949, 167).

The salaries these female employees received were also lower than those received by male employees. The March 1940 minutes of the meeting of the Board of Managers of the New Jersey Reformatory for Women stated:

> Our cottage officers work practically twenty-four hours a day and receive from $50 to $70 a month plus maintenance. Male guards in the reformatories for men work eight hours and receive a minimum of $150 per month.

Cottage officers were officially on twelve-hour shifts at this time. However, they still lived and ate in the cottages, so the homelike atmosphere with the staff providing good parental role models conducive to reform was carried on. It was not until 1951, in New Jersey, that the shift to an eight-hour day was made, and the requirement to live in the cottages was relaxed.

In 1955, the annual Budget Request for the New Jersey Reformatory for Women pointed out that the salary range for a male correctional officer was $3,480 to $4,380, while the range for a female cottage supervisor Gr. II, was between $2,520 and $3,120. In 1965, female cottage officers were finally paid on the same scale as male correctional officers. This was undoubtedly because three male correctional officers were assigned to the closed security cottage in 1962.

Recognition of limited opportunities and salary inequities for women in the corrections field are documented in the newsletters of the Women's Correctional Association during the 1960s. In the November 1965 Newsletter, Iverne R. Carter, superintendent of the California Institution for Women, wrote:

> Those of us interested in providing developmental opportunities for line or middle management staff are aware of the limited areas of professional exposure available. While most states and the federal government have numerous institutions for men in order to give employees potential exposure to various administrative and treatment techniques, this kind of transfer opportunity is not available to women generally. In California there has been limited opportunity to transfer correctional counselors from the field and men's institutions into women's institutions and vice versa. There has been no opportunity for employees in other areas.

Margaret Morrissey, superintendent of the State Reformatory for Women in Dwight, Illinois, reported in the April 1967 Newsletter:

> Effective February 1, 1967, the positions of Warden I and II have been abolished. These employees have been reclassified as Correctional Officers by the State Civil Service Commission, with a salary range of $355 to $515, with midpoint salary of $430 after three years.

The impact of the women's movement that commenced in the middle 1960s was felt by women working in the corrections field, and efforts to bring about change were heightened.

Pressures for Change: 1970 - 1990

The 1960s and 1970s witnessed major social changes that were felt by all parts of society, including the criminal justice system. The civil rights movement was translated in corrections to inmates' rights. This, combined with the women's movement, highlighted vast inequities in the treatment of adult and juvenile females in conflict with the law, as well as inequities in opportunities and salaries for women working at all levels of the criminal justice system.

Both public and private sectors of society became involved in measures aimed at increasing occupational opportunities in corrections for all minorities and women. These included the 1972 amendments to Title VII of the 1964 Civil Rights Act, the Joint Commission on Correctional Manpower and Training, The National Advisory Commission on Criminal Justice Standards and Goals, and the American Correctional Association (Morton 1981).

Morton (1981, 10) reported the following from a national survey she conducted in 1979 on the employment of women correctional officers:

> The overriding reason given for hiring women was Title VII of the Civil Rights Act . . . The other responses were, in order of importance, as follows:
>
> - meeting some need on the part of the system, such as to search female visitors
> - the receipt of qualified applicants
> - the expansion of the work force, which made such action more acceptable
> - the shortage of male applicants

In 1975 at the American Correctional Association's Annual Congress, a Women's Caucus met "to address the concerns of women in corrections." As a result of a Women's Caucus recommendation to the ACA President in 1978, a Task Force on Women as a subcommittee of the Affirmative Action Committee of ACA was mandated. The purpose of the Task Force "was to address itself to the unique position of women working in the field of corrections both in the United States and Canada, identify areas of concern as well as opportunity, and develop support systems for women within the field" (Nicolai 1982).

In 1981 the Task Force on Women broadened its goals "to enhance the recognition, participation, and utilization of women professionals within ACA (as well as) throughout the correctional field."

The Task Force on Women has met continuously at annual congresses since 1978. Members have contributed articles to ACA's newsletter, *On the Line*, arranged sessions pertinent to women's concerns at every annual and winter meeting, sponsored policy statements, and submitted recommendations to

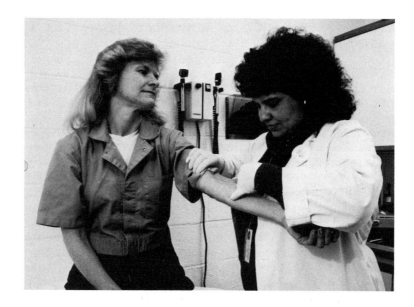

the ACA Nominating Committee. It has worked through state chapters to increase the membership of women in ACA and has provided a networking and support system for women working in the field of corrections.

There is no question that the efforts to increase the participation of women throughout correctional organizations and systems in the past two decades have made a significant impact. In 1983 women made up 11.5 percent of the ACA membership. In 1990 this was approximately 28 percent. (ACA Membership Department cautions these statistics are based on the number of members providing this information at the time of joining, not the total membership.) At the 1990 Annual Congress of Correction, women were sworn in as president, vice president, and treasurer of the Association. Women make up 48 percent of the Board of Governors and 47 percent of the Delegate Assembly (Travisono, A. P. 1990, 1).

The increase in the percentage of women working in the correctional field has grown from 12 percent in 1969 to approximately 23 percent in 1978 (Morton 1981) to 30 percent in 1988 (Travisono, D. 1989, 3). Today women work throughout correctional systems. Lynn Zimmer states, "Prior to 1972, virtually no women worked as correctional officers in men's prisons; today women supervise male inmates in every state prison system as well as the Federal Bureau of Prisons and most county jails" (1989, 55). A number of women serve as wardens of male prisons.

The Forgotten Offender

While the number of women working in the corrections field was growing, the 1980s witnessed a growth in female inmates at all levels of government at a significantly higher rate than that of male inmates. In spite of this rate of growth, women still make up only about 5 percent of the total adult inmate population in the United States. During the 1950s, 1960s, and 1970s, women made up 3 to 4 percent of the inmate population (Simon 1975).

The American Correctional Association's survey (1990) on female offenders found the major change in characteristics that had occurred in the past decade was the increased number who have a dependency on alcohol or drugs. Other than this increase, the offense characteristics have changed very little for women. They continue to be committed in large numbers for property offenses—larceny, thefts, and moral order offenses—prostitution, and commercialized vice. The violent crime rate of women has increased very little in the past several decades.

The large majority of these incarcerated women reported that they had been physically or sexually abused. A significant number had attempted suicide or other self-injurious behavior. A similar finding was reported in Canada's Task Force Report of Federally Sentenced Women (Creating Choices 1990). Additionally, over 60 percent of the adult female inmates were single parents who were caring for their children prior to incarceration.

The surveys on state and local government facilities housing women found that only 25 percent reported having a classification system geared to women. Classification systems developed and implemented for male offenders have not been validated as significantly predictive for women offenders.

Staffing Female Programs

On the average, 82 percent of the local facilities housing women and 51 percent of state facilities are administered by men. The staff are, on the average, 44 percent male in local facilities and 37 percent male in state facilities. It is not unusual today to find women administrators and staff of female institutions who have had the majority of their prior correctional experience in all-male institutions. As has been previously pointed out, many more women are working throughout correctional systems today. Since there are so few women inmates to work with relative to the number of male inmates, these women gain their experience in all-male institutions. This is particularly critical for women offenders since the surveys found that state and local correctional systems offered very little specialized training for working with women inmates.

As a result, the female institutions are custody driven, as are the institutions for men, and the majority are designed and run on the male model. The surveys found that new facilities to house women inmates both on the local and state levels are designed for medium or maximum security. Very few are designed for minimum security, prerelease, or community alternatives. This is true in spite of the fact that there is no evidence that women offenders exhibit more violent behavior today than in the past. Their crimes are still largely morals charges and petty thefts.

Challenge for Women In Correctional Employment

One hundred years ago, women's groups in the community as well as individual women of prominence and influence lobbied for and oversaw the development and running of women's reformatories. More recently, the reform movement of the 1960s was abandoned in the late 1980s and early 1990s in the face of limited financial resources and the lack of interest in the female offender. The women's movement of the 1980s and 1990s has turned to more middle-class personal goals of pro-choice, maternity leave, etc., for mainstream women and has turned away from the dispossessed and the casualties of society.

Female offenders have no base of power from which to operate. Women in correctional employment, whether in the public or private sector, have had to work hard to help themselves, so it is not surprising that they've lost touch with the female offender. They, with the American Correctional Association and other professional associations, must now take up the challenge to bring about equity for the treatment of female offenders, and, most important, lead the way in creating innovative alternative programs that will keep female offenders from the overburdened male model institutions.

Canada has already started. Their Task Force on Federally Sentenced Women, lead by a woman, with members from the public and private sectors as well as female offenders, recommended closing the Prison for Women at Kingston, Ontario, within four years and developing regional facilities throughout the country. With approval from the government in the fall of 1990, the implementation of this is under way.

The United States must look at their model and set their own course. It is, however, safe to say that the problems of female offenders cannot be solved—and indeed may not even be addressed—in the future without the interest, advocacy, and leadership of women in correctional employment.

References

American Correctional Association. 1990. *The female offender: What does the future hold?* Laurel, Md.: American Correctional Association.

Close, Kathryn. 1949. Reform without locks. *Survey* (March): 163-168.

Correctional Service Canada. 1990. *Creating choices: The report of the Task Force on Federally Sentenced Women.* Ottawa: CSC.

Freedman, Estelle B. *Their sister's keepers.* 1981. Ann Arbor, Mich.: University of Michigan Press.

Morton, Joann B. 1981. Women in correctional employment: where are they now and where are they headed? In *Women in Corrections,* 7-16. College Park, Md.: American Correctional Association.

Nicolai, Sandra. 1980. Synopsis and history of American Correctional Association Task Force on Women. Paper appended to Minutes Midwinter Meeting, ACA Task Force on Women, January 26, 1982.

Rafter, Nicole Hahn. 1990. *Partial justice, women, prisons, and social control.* 2d ed. New Brunswick, N.J.: Transaction Publishers.

Simon, Rita J. 1975. *The contemporary woman and crime.* Rockville, Md.: National Institute of Mental Health.

Travisono, A. P. 1990. Leading the way in equality. *On the Line* 13. September: 1.

Travisono, Diana N., ed. 1989. *Vital statistics in corrections.* Laurel, Md.: American Correctional Association.

Wines, E. C., ed. 1871. *Transactions of the National Congress on Penitentiary and Reformatory Discipline held at Cincinnati, Ohio, October 12-18, 1870.* Albany, N.Y.: Weed, Parsons and Company.

Zimmer, Lynn. 1989. Solving women's employment problems in corrections: Shifting the burden to administrators. *Women in Criminal Justice* 1:55-79.

What Does the Future Hold?

Joann B. Morton, D.P.A.

While no one can predict the future with complete accuracy, there are certain trends and issues that have the potential to affect women's role in correctional employment in future years. These trends include general observations about corrections roles as an instrument of social control and the nature of the work force in the coming years. Also, system and individual factors that can influence the full integration of women in the workplace will be explored.

The Year 2000 and Beyond

As the year 2000 approaches, popular and academic literature is being flooded with ideas about what the future will bring. Since correctional organizations are a reflection of societal and governmental policies and practices, an overview of some of the more significant trends appears to be in order.

First, there is no indication that society's views on crime or criminals will become any less punitive in the future. The country as a whole is growing older, and fear of crime is not abating. The so-called "War on Drugs" has flooded the correctional system with a wide variety of offenders, and there appear to be few positive programs geared toward eliminating the myriad of social ills driving people to seek solace in drugs and alcohol (Hirschel & Keny 1990). Only a few voices are being heard that challenge the concept that the criminal justice system should be the first line of defense in the battle for social control. These factors portend the continued growth of correctional populations, which in 1990 had reached an all-time high (ACA 1991). The trends toward expanding mandatory sentences, longer sentences, and an overreliance on institutionalization show no signs of abating in the near future. It appears that corrections will continue to be a growth industry into the twenty-first century.

Accompanying this trend is the fact that the growing scarcity of economic resources will continue to plague most governmental units. While economic up-and-down turns will continue, overall the national debt and resistance to increased taxation will limit the funds available for governmental spending. Already legislators find themselves making hard choices of whether to fund education, public health, or correc-

111

tions. Increasingly, corrections will find that any manpower savings made through the application of technological advances and new equipment are overcome by sheer numbers of offenders. Workloads will continue to be high, and innovation without resources will be a challenge.

The demographic changes already influencing the work force are the leading edge of an encouraging trend toward increased correctional employment for women. These changes will become even more intense, and by the year 2000 women and minorities will be the numerical majority in the work force (Naisbitt & Aburdene 1990). Employing women will become a necessity mandated by the shortage of qualified men. Legislative mandates and judicial rulings will become less important reasons for hiring women. Agencies will be forced to seek them out if positions are to be filled. The voluntary hiring of women may help eliminate some of the overt hostility and discrimination that have occurred in the past. It will not, however, ensure a fully integrated work force or the maximum use of women's talents and productivity.

Making it Work

Full integration of women into the correctional work force will require a continuation of a number of changes some agencies are currently exploring. These changes will have to begin at the top of the organization. Future administrators will have to support the concept of full use of all employees regardless of gender and seek ways to make it happen. They will have to prove by actions as well as words that sexual harassment will not be tolerated. The "boys will be boys" attitude will become outdated as the economic consequences of investing in recruiting and training women only to have them hounded out of their jobs becomes more evident. Attitudes of older and less secure employees may be difficult to change, but their behavior on the job can be addressed.

Organizational policies, procedures, and practices will have to be examined on an ongoing basis. Administrators will not be able to assume that because written policy and procedures provide for full use of women employees that it is in fact happening. Management audits, informal discussion sessions with employees at all levels of the organization, and formal and informal complaint mechanisms will have to be in place.

Administrators will have to remember that "same" and "equal" are not synonymous terms. "Same" means to conform in every respect; "equal" means identical in value (Bartolo 1991). Competent managers treat all employees equally—that is, of identical value to the tasks at hand. Positive, productive managers will have to supervise increasingly heterogeneous work forces in such a way that employees' individual strengths are maximized and their weaknesses minimized.

Training will be needed to help employees overcome skill or knowledge deficiencies they might have in completing the tasks to be performed. The concept of "we train everybody the same" will become passe. Women will be trained according to their needs and expected to perform the full range of duties relative to all positions.

The issue of privacy will continue to require attention but by necessity will have to be narrowly defined. Increased professionalism of staff, treatment of necessary intrusive procedures with sensitivity, and continued expansion of physical plant modifications will bring about improved conditions for all.

To compete for and retain qualified female employees, correctional agencies will have to address job-related issues such as single parent households and child care availability. Responsibilities outside work for all employees will have to be considered when making assignments. Some agencies have already established employee child care programs on-site, and the National Institute of Corrections awarded demonstration grants in 1991 to develop and assess employee child care programs.

While these and other activities will be initiated to attract more female employees, they will enhance the correctional workplace of all employees. Opening up organizations and enhancing staff opportunities to maximize their potential and contributions will ensure that corrections attracts and retains the quantity and quality of work force required.

There is no question that women's role in corrections is going to expand at all levels. In 1990, a record number of state prison systems—Alaska, North Dakota, South Dakota, and Puerto Rico—were headed by women. Numerous state and local probation, parole, and juvenile service systems were directed by women. Increasing numbers of women will continue to move into supervisory, management, and leadership roles in correctional agencies and related areas such as professional associations.

This expansion will be enhanced if women examine their career choices carefully and choose rather than stumble into correctional employment. As women move into the field, they will need to establish positive working relationships with other women and support each other. Society often encourages competition among women, but in the world of work networking is one of the keys to success. Women in leadership roles will have the responsibility of serving as role models and mentors for those entering the system. No one can succeed in corrections or any other field without help from others. While men will also serve as role models and mentors, women have experiences unique to their gender and will be in a position to help other women deal with issues of working in what will continue to be a nontraditional environment for them.

Finally, to successfully integrate into correctional systems in the future, women will have to find common ground to work together with their male counterparts. Through identification of mutual problems and concerns and the joint resolution of these issues, the work environment of all will be improved and the effectiveness and efficiency of correctional agencies will be more successfully attained.

Women as correctional employees have the potential to continue to enhance and enrich the future of corrections. Their successful integration and the maximum use of their resources will require a combined effort of men and women throughout corrections and the continued expansion of knowledge through additional research and study. Corrections cannot afford to do otherwise.

References

American Correctional Association. 1991. *Juvenile and adult correctional departments, institutions, agencies and paroling authorities.* Laurel, Md.: ACA.

Bartolo, A. 1991. *The female offender in the Bureau of Prisons.* Paper presented at the Issues in Corrections Federal Bureau of Prisons, Female Offenders, Washington, D.C.

Hirschel, J. D., & J. R. Keny. 1990. Outpatient treatment for substance-abusing offenders. In *Clinical Treatment of the Criminal Offender,* pp. 111-129. New York: Haworth.

Naisbitt, J., & P. Aburdene. 1990. *Megatrends 2000.* New York: William Morrow and Company.

Contributors

William C. Collins, J.D., is co-founder and co-editor of the *Correctional Law Reporter,* a journal of correctional legal issues written for the correctional administrator. He also consults extensively regarding legal issues in corrections.

The Honorable Helen G. Corrothers began her career in corrections when she left her position as a captain in the United States Army and was appointed warden of the Women's Correctional Facility in Arkansas. In 1983 she was appointed by President Reagan to the U. S. Parole Commission and in 1985 was selected by him to serve on the U.S. Sentencing Commission. In 1990 she became president of the American Correctional Association.

Rose Etheridge was a research specialist at the Preventive Services Institute of the University of North Carolina School of Social Work at the time of publication of the article "Female Employees in All-male Correctional Facilities" in 1984, portions of the which are used in "Working in a Nontraditional Environment."

Cynthia Hale, co-author of the 1984 article, "Female Employees in All-male Correctional Facilities," was an instructor at the Bureau of Prison's Staff Training Academy in Glynco, Georgia, at the time of its publication. Portions of the article are used in this publication.

Margaret Hambrick was deputy assistant director of Education/Recreation/Vocational Training for the Bureau of Prisons in Washington, D. C., at the time of publication of the article "Female Employees in All-male Correctional Facilities," which she co-authored with Etheridge and Hale in 1984. She is currently warden of the Federal Correctional Institution in Lexington, Kentucky.

Mary Hawkes has a doctorate in sociology with a concentration in criminology from Boston University. She began her career in corrections as a classification officer at the New Jersey Reformatory for Women in the late 1950s. She was a professor of sociology at Rhode Island College until 1989. She presently serves on numerous boards of directors of criminal justice agencies in the Boston area.

Perry Johnson's distinguished career with the Michigan Department of Corrections included twelve years as that agency's head. He is currently a corrections consultant and in 1992 will begin a two-year term as president of the American Correctional Association.

Barbara Jones received her degree from the University of Kentucky, College of Law. She has been involved with correctional litigations since November 1978. Since December 1981, she has served as General Counsel for the Kentucky Corrections Cabinet. In January 1989, she successfully defended a correctional case before the United States Supreme Court.

Jess Maghan, Ph.D., is associate commissioner of Training and Resource Development for the New York City Department of Correction. He has an extensive background in performance technology, instructional development, and the impact of social and psychological sciences in public sector training.

Leasa McLeish-Blackwell, M. P. A., is a training development specialist with the Correction Academy of the City of New York. She holds a Bachelor of Arts degree from The City University of New York and a Masters of Public Administration from C.W. Post University. She has an extensive background in law enforcement and correctional services.

About the Editor

Joann B. Morton, D.P.A., an associate professor at the College of Criminal Justice, South Carolina, holds a doctorate in public administration from the University of Georgia. She is a noted lecturer and consultant on issues including correctional policy and management, special needs offenders, and women as correctional employees. Her research on issues involving women in correctional employment began in the early 1970s and has involved publications, presentations, and the development of national correctional policy statements on women and professional leadership of their ratification by the American Correctional Association. She is a recipient of the ACA's E. R. Cass Award for achievement in corrections.